CW01465587

35 EARACHE YEARS OF NOISE

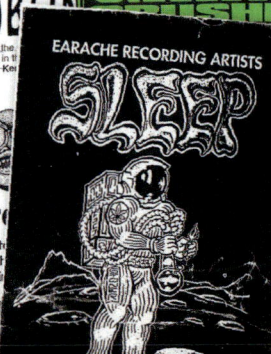

HELLBASTARD

Garden of Shadows

For your FREE bookshelf slipcase suitable for hosting the full set of all 5
Pathologist's Report titles – simply email your NAME and POSTAL ADDRESS

iboughtall5@earache.com

Thanks for supporting Carcass and Earache

EARACHE EXTREMITY EXPERIMENT

EUROPEAN TOUR JUNE 2004

ACCESS ALL AREAS

AAA HAUNTED MEAN FIDD 05/05/07

DOS U.K. £1.50

CONCRETE SOX

onslaught

SCUM DRIBBLERS

HERESY

NAPALM DEATH

A THRASH EXTRAVAGANZA

MORBID ANGEL

exploitatinment?

pitch shifter
INFOTAINMENT

earache '98 nextgen

DECAPITATED

Rotting Christ

I HATE MUSIC

0990 243003 BT

MORBID ANGEL

VIP
ACCESS ALL AREAS

NAPALM DEATH

diatribes ✦ world tour 1996

The Stargate Opens 9.9.96

Misery

ULTRAVIOLENT

Morbid Angel
Covenant

IRON MONKEY

versus

ACRIMONY

AT THE OLD ANGEL
Nottingham
Friday 6th September
£2.00/2.50 (STUDENTS)

-PITCH SHIFTER
DRILL

8 SOUTHAMPTON - JOINERS
9 LONDON - UNDERWORLD
10 LEEDS - DUCHESS OF YORK
11 LIVERPOOL - ROYAL COURT
12 GLASGOW - KING TUT'S
13 EDINBURGH - MUSIC BOX
MANCHESTER - ROCK WORLD
15 CAMBRIDGE - T.B.C.
HARLOW - SQUARE
DERBY - THE WHEREHOUSE
NEWCASTLE - RIVERSIDE

RIVERSIDE PROMOTIONS PRESENTS

EVENT: AT THE GATES

THE BERZERKER
World of Lies

CATHEDRAL

MELKWEG
21.11.76
ACCESS

The Gates

dub war
wrong side of beautiful

MADMAN IS ABSOLUTE HAPPYFACE

Access All Areas

ACOUSTIC SHOW
london - borderline café
TUESDAY AUGUST 20 '96

GUEST

access all area photo

CON
THE CON
NOVE
MYSPA

access all area

date 05/10

band CULT of

GUSTO INC. PRESENTS
FROM HOUSTON

PAIN TEENS
FROM JAPAN

BOREDOMS
FROM NEW YORK CITY

BRUTAL TRUTH

MON.
MAY 31

ADVANCE TICKETS ONLY

ORANGE GOBLIN

IRON MONKEY

+ Dark Her

GRIND CRUSHER

EARACHE RECORDING ARTISTS

SLEEP

HEAD POUNDING TRA

NAPALM DEATH
EXTRA PAIN RECEIVING INGREDIENT

METAL HAMMER

END OF TOUR

COMING NEXT WICKED WORLD

corporation
187

Garden of Shadows

LEEDS
STAGE ACCESS
LOCK UP
MUNICIPAL WASTE
LEEDS

BLACK SABBATH
WORLD TOUR
THE END
GUEST

LIVE NATION
NOTTINGHAM RC
RIVAL SONS
13/04/15 | Authorised by | LN
ACCESS ALL AREAS

XMAS BASH
RIVAL SONS
EVILE
SAVAGE MESSIAH
AAA
ACCESS ALL AREAS
LADY STARLIGHT
REBEL L
@ISLINGTON ELECTROWERKZ
FRIDAY DECEMBER 9TH 2011

ROCK
OF HONOUR
Welcomes
Dan Tobin

LIVE NATION
MAIDEN BARFLY
BLACKBERRY SMOKE
11.13 | Authorised by | SB
ACCESS ALL AREAS
GUEST AFTER SHOW PHOTO

THE LONG ROAD HO...
HIS DEBUT SOLO ALBUM

AAA
MW
Rescue
14/12
DhP Group

AAA
Evile
R/C
21/1

BLACKBERRY SMOKE
TOURING
KEEP ON KEEPIN' ON
Notts
AAA 23/6

BLACKBERRY SMOKE

KAGOULE

METROPOLIS
MUSIC
MUNICIPAL WASTE
B'HAM ACADEMY 2
3/02/08
A.A.A.

BITERS

ELECTRIC BLOOD
TOUR 2015

LIVE NATION
Venue
Artiste
Date | Authorised by
ACCESS ALL AREAS
VIP STA...

Blackberry Smoke
Holding all the Roses

029470
029470
STAFF/PERFOR...
TICKET IS ONLY VALID FOR THE PERSON NAMED
PHOTO ID REQUIRED

LIVE NATION
Venue Les
Artiste 7TH
Authoris...

FANTOUR
2008

KERRANG! TOUR 2008
SUM 41
Frank Carter
& THE RATTLESNAKES
ROAM
BITERS
AAA

BITERS
EUROPEAN TOUR
WINTER 2016
AAA

Live Nation
presents
BLACKBERRY SMOKE
Venue: The Bodega
Saturday 01 March 14
Over 14s only
Doors 19:00
Standing
£14.00
£14.00 In Adv
48
01 Mar 14
48
alt-tickets.co.uk

029470
Dan Tobin
Artist Blackberry Smoke
LUKE PIPER
AVALON & GLADE
Authorised by
Michael ...
GREENPEACE WaterAid OXFAM

LIVE NATION
Venue CAMDEN BARFLY
Artiste BLACKBERRY SMOKE
Date 13.11.13 | Authorised by SB
ACCESS ALL AREAS

Devastating Death Metal
the way it should be:
blunt, brutal and
bastard heavy.

VIP
Evile

ION
PREADS
2010
EANO

DEICIDE

ANNIHILATOR

MORT...

GOTHMINISTER
deadfilmstar
04.19 · Nottingham · Rock city
04.20 · Bristol · Bierkeller
04.21 · Glasgow · Cathouse
04.22 · Bradford · Rios
04.23 · Camberley · Agincourt Rock Venue
04.25 · Liverpool · Barfly
04.27 · Norwich · Waterfront
04.28 · Sheffield · Corporation
04.29 · London · Underworld
04.30 · Manchester · Satans hollow
FOR UPDATES VISIT

ARTIST
SONISPHERE
DATES: 31-Jul-2010
ON STAGE Bonemia
NAME Enforcer
BAND Enforcer
DRESSING ROOMS | PRODUCTION

AAA

mean fiddler

Rival Sons
13/7/11
BL

LIVE NATION
Venue FORUM
Artiste RIVAL SONS
Date 6DEC14 | Authorised by SX
ACCESS ALL AREAS
VIP STAFF GUEST AFTER SHOW PHOTO

LIVE NATION
Venue SOTON GUILDHALL
Artiste RIVAL SONS
Date 4/4/15 | Authorised by JC
ACCESS ALL AREAS

behemoth
SUPREME LORD
DMORTE...
Demigod tour 13.01.2005 - 22.01.20...

ALL ACCESS

EARACHE REC.
bitor
BERLIN 2004
MM
Vickerstaff
nien

RIVAL SONS
ライヴァル・サンズ
すべてを凌駕する圧倒的な存在感 ロック史上に残る傑作!!
RIVAL SONS
NEW ALBUM「HEAD DOWN」
HYDRANT MUSIC

FOREWORD

WHENEVER SEPULTURA WOULD PLAY IN NOTTINGHAM-UK'S
ROCK CITY! DIGBY WOULD SHOW UP WITH EARACHE
BOXES! IT WAS LIKE FUCKING CHRISTMAS! ON THOSE
BOXES I DISCOVER PUDGE TUNNEL AND GOD FLESH
AMONG MANY OTHERS! TO PUT IT SIMPLE EARACHE IN
THE 90'S WAS THE SHIT! THE UNDERGROUND WAS
ON FIRE, ENTOMBED, TERRORIZER, CARCASS, NAPALM
DEATH AND I ALWAYS LOVED THE EARACHE LOGO
DESIGN BY JEFF WALKER ~~WHO~~ (CARCASS) WHO WOULD
LATER DESIGN THE LOGO FOR "GO AHEAD AND DIE"
LONG LIVE THE UNDERGROUND, LONG LIVE EARACHE!!!

MAX CAVALERA
Soulfly/Cavalera Conspiracy

Until a few years ago, I ran a blog called Ask Earache, designed to answer fan questions about the label, the idea being to de-mystify the inner workings of an Indie Metal/Rock Label, plus I wanted to jot down my own memories and thoughts of how things were going as the label progressed from 2005-2015.

Continuing on from that idea, this book is the story of Earache Records as recounted first hand by the Earache staffers, fans and friends in the industry who chime in with their thoughts on how a little DIY affair from Nottingham made it to global prominence as a long-standing and respected, cutting-edge label.

Key people explain how the chaos unfolded and what it was like to see the explosion of the very first 'extreme metal' bands, who went from the DIY underground tape-trading scene to now rightly being considered pioneers in the genre of their own making.

Discovering and promoting new acts was our strength, but we also had our share of flops and calamities, illustrating how running any label is very much a hit and miss affair, but the core strength of our longevity is adapting to the changes that come along, often when you least expect it.

Earache: 35 Years of Noise shows the label in two parts:

1) The extreme metal revolution of our eardrum-shattering first 100-odd releases, complete with the excursions away from that core sound - the dalliance with Hard Techno and Ragga-Metal as a precursor to Nu-Metal, and our complete swerving away from Black Metal explained.

2) The sudden A&R policy switch to Rock N Roll - which occurred on Boxing Day 2010 - the day I signed and began to build a career for Rival Sons, who quickly became our most successful artist in decades. Blues-based Rock N Roll was where my own tastes in music were heading, prompted by Lemmy referring to Motörhead as a Rock N Roll band (not Metal as I assumed). That made me explore and appreciate the roots of Metal, coming from the Blues, a looser, groovier more dynamic style of Rock genuinely seemed fresh and appealed so much that the label headed exclusively into that territory, single-mindedly seeking out the newest bands playing Rock N Roll - while the naysayers and onlookers despairingly concluded we'd gone "Pub Rock".

Coinciding with the switch however, over 20 Earache titles have entered the UK Top 40 which is not too shabby, especially given the first 25 years doing the Extreme stuff, we never even bothered the chart compilers.

In thirty-five years, we now boast a catalogue over 700 releases deep, and be it Extreme Metal or Rock N Roll, you can be sure that every single one of our albums was carefully signed, carefully curated and promoted and marketed with mad energy and love. Hopefully you'll find a cool story about your favourite bands inside.

Earache remains founder-owned and running the ship on a daily basis is very unusual in the modern Music Industry, it gives me the freedom to sign what I like - it's Trap currently - and time will tell whether it's another failed excursion or a bold move.

Lastly, I hope you enjoy this book. Thank you to everyone who contributed their stories to this tome, cheers to the fans for your support and rock on!

DIGBY PEARSON
April 2022

Morbid Angel

CONTENTS

WRITTEN BY: Guy Strachan and Dave Ling

WITH CONTRIBUTIONS FROM: Al Dawson, Andy Copping, Barney Greenway, Benji Webbe, Brit Turner, Charlie Starr, Dan Hardingham, Dan Tobin, David Vincent, Digby Pearson, Gaz Jennings, Gizz Butt, Glen Benton, Håvard Ellefsen (Mortiis), Hugh Jones, Jake Smith, Jeff Walker, Jeni Lambert, Joaquim Ghirotti, Johannes Persson, Jon Barry, Kevin Sharp, Laurent Merle, Lee Dorrian , Max Cavalera, Mick Harris, Mitch Dickinson, Ol Drake, Paul Ryan, Paul Sayer, Pete Lee, Rasyid Juraimi, Sam Bean, Scott Holiday, Shane Embury, Steve Watson, Tom Hadfield, Tomas Lindberg

Design & Layout by Lewis-Jon Somerscales @ Zero Three Two Creative

Carcass

BRAINBOX POLLUTION PROMOTIONS PRESENTS...

CARCASS
BOLT THROWER
ENTOMBED
From Sweden; UK debut

THURSDAY 15TH MARCH

THE BOSTON,178, JUNCTION ROAD, LONDON,N19.(OPP. TUFNELL PK.)£4 ADVANCE £5 DOORS(£4.50 CONCS.). FROM 7-11.30PM TICKETS FROM SHADES, RHYTHM, ROUGH TRADE, VINYL EXPERIENCE, VINYL SOLUTION...INF:01 272 6921

Al Dawson

42, HAZELWOOD RD. NOTTINGHAM NG7 5LB U.K.

CHAPTER ONE

DIY DAYS/ BEDROOM LABEL

While it's true that most books about British independent music focus on the likes of Alan McGee's Creation Records, Daniel Miller's Mute, Ivo Watts-Russel and 4AD and Tony Wilson's Factory, many other label owners have employed a similar ethos; a deep-seated obsession with music, a fanatical belief in the records that they released and, perhaps most importantly, they have gathered together a stable of like-minded artists, staff and fans who strongly identify with 'their' label to the point where they could, would and do call it a home.

Some of these labels lasted a few years, others have continued to the present day. Ron Johnson, Postcard and Sarah have their reputations curated, fostered and bolstered decades after their respective demise. By the same token, one label founder that has managed to stay the course for thirty-five years is Digby Pearson.

"WE'RE A HOME FOR THOSE THAT DON'T PLAY THE GAME THE WAY YOU'RE TOLD TO."

While his Earache label bears one the most varied catalogues within the independent world, its name remains synonymous with the extreme end of metal. Looking at the range of artists that Earache have signed, from Napalm Death, Carcass, Godflesh, Bolt Thrower and Entombed, to Dub War, Scorn, Mortiis, to Deicide and Municipal Waste, through to Rival Sons and Blackberry Smoke, all those bands came to the label from different influences and different places.

Likewise, the staffers featured in this book all came from different backgrounds. Each discovered the label in different ways, but all felt drawn to Earache. Having been treated as

Rudimentary Peni

Al and Pushead

Dig with Heresy

Slayer at The Marquee

somewhere between an irreverence and a joke by the industry at large for so many years (as an example, there are few, if any references to the label in any of the histories of British independent labels on the bookshelves), Earache's contribution to independent music was finally recognised in 2015 when Pearson received the Pioneer Award at the Association Of Independent Music awards ceremony.

"We don't sign what's popular, or what the current formula [for success] is, and we don't sign any old project, because we know the ingredients it has to have to work with us," says former Earache employee Dan Tobin. "We're like a home for all the misfits and oddballs, those that don't play the game the way you're told to, and I like that. The way we have always operated is that it is everything or nothing. We want and we need each band or release to work otherwise we lose money and potentially we go out of business. So you have to make the right decisions, and often as well as the music, for us it's about the kind of artist we are dealing with – they need to be on our wavelength, so to speak. So those early bands, like Napalm Death or Morbid Angel or whatever were definitely cut from the same cloth as Dig in thoughts, work ethic, ambitions, and ideology."

One common reference point that Earache has with the more well-known names of Mute and Creation is that it was punk, whether in music or by attitude (or both), that provided the catalyst for their respective label owners to connect with music in a big way even if, in Pearson's case, he had hitherto displayed precious little interest in anything musical at all.

"I wasn't really into music when I was in my early teens," is the surprising admission from Dig. "I was really into sports; football, cricket, table tennis, any sport I could play really; music never really entered into my head."

However, in November 1977, the manager of Pearson's local Virgin Records store in Nottingham was prosecuted for obscenity after displaying the sleeve to The Sex Pistols' 'Never Mind The Bollocks' in the shop window. The ensuing controversy was enough to entice him into the shop to purchase said album.

"It was the first record that I ever bought, although I may also have bought an LP by Tangerine Dream on the same day!" he laughs. "I had to buy a record player as well, as we didn't have one in the house!"

Following this epiphany, Dig began gravitating towards the left-field, fringe material such as Crass, Killing Joke and Rudimentary Peni – all so beloved of the late John Peel, who in time would prove to be a key figure in the early success of Earache. "A magical world of music opened up to me because of BBC radio, taping every John Peel show, then discovering Tommy Vance, starting my love of Heavy Metal. I quickly became a music obsessive."

Yet it was the second wave of punk bands that sprung up as the 1980s beckoned, Discharge and Motörhead in particular (because they mixed the speed of punk with the power of metal), that captured Dig's attention, and he began booking shows, playing in bands, producing fanzines and networking with like-minded souls across the globe. His growing fascination with the business side of the music industry set him apart from many of his friends, who grew so familiar with Dig's knowledge of the subject that they christened him with the nickname of 'EMI'!

Heavily involved with the scene on an increasingly international basis and with a resulting slew of contacts for bands and distributors, the next logical step was for Dig to start his own record label. Having quit university, being unemployed and therefore impoverished, he took to releasing flexi discs in lieu of full-blown vinyl. Three such flexis were produced; two international compilations, one featured Dig's faves, Ipswich skate-hardcore heroes The Stupids, and the third an EP by local ultra-fast hardcore ragers Heresy.

With encouragement from Americans such as Pushead from Septic Death, who released a seminal hardcore punk compilation 'Cleanse The Bacteria' boasting three future Earache label managers listed on the back credits, and later known as the man behind some of the key Metallica art, moves were made into pressing up proper vinyl LPs; piggybacking onto Bristol label Children Of The Revolution for distribution, the first album was the European release of 'The Return Of Martha Splatterhead' by The Accused, in turn rapidly followed by a split album between the more local Concrete Sox and Heresy.

Though he hated the Conservatives, Pearson engaged in the practice of almost every indie musician and label owner at the time of signing onto the UK's then-Tory government's Enterprise Allowance Scheme, a ruse aimed at massaging down the high levels of unemployment of the day, allowing people to set up their own businesses, effectively signing off the dole but still getting dole money as a weekly wage for two years. As a result he could devote all of his time to the label, seeking out the fastest, heaviest bands around, aiming to match what he witnessed at Slayer's Marquee show in London in 1985, a pivotal

Picture by Jenny Plaits

Dig with Heresy/Concrete Sox at Hazelwood Road flat.

Letter from Euronymous / Mayhem

Napalm Death

Damian Thompson / Sacrilege

moment for the scene.

The album released as MOSH 3, Napalm Death's 'Scum' upped the ante far beyond the 'speed metal' of the time, and threw the label both a financial lifeline and wider prominence, it also began the upward trajectory of Napalm Death to levels of popularity that no-one had ever dreamed of being possible. 'Scum' quickly caught the ear of influential BBC deejay John Peel who promptly began playing tracks from the album in heavy rotation and bringing the band in for their first Peel Session – all the more surprising when it's borne in mind that tapes of the A-Side tracks had been making the rounds for several months with scant interest anywhere.

"Daz [Russell, a local gig promoter of shows at the legendary Mermaid pub] gave us £120 which paid for an eight-hour booking with an engineer," remembers drummer Mick Harris. "We chose Mike Ivory because of what he'd done with Sacrilege and we felt he'd understand what we wanted. Damian from Sacrilege lent Justin his MXR distortion pedal because Justin really liked that Sacrilege tone."

Session complete, the results were scheduled to form a split release with Atavistic, but this project fizzled out without trace. Electing to hold onto the tapes, copies were sent out to a number of labels and individuals such as Manic Ears, Children Of The Revolution and Pushead of Septic Death. There was little, if any interest in the results, until Dig enquired about the recordings. ►

Intense Degree

The Stupids

Al Dawson

Dig in early Earache HQ

"Yeah, there was no great ambition or fanfare with that album," Dig recalls. "That record was in limbo, they recorded it and no-one wanted to release it. Justin [Broadrick, the band's guitarist] had touted the tapes around with no joy, so he just sold the tapes to me. Because there weren't enough tracks to release a full LP, I set about getting the new line-up signed and into the studio. Well, there was a hand-typed two-page agreement.

"Three thousand copies were pressed and I can remember having my fingers crossed when it came out hoping that people would buy it because if they didn't, I was fucked," admits Dig. "I'd put everything I had into it! A week later, our distributors called and said that they needed more copies as they'd sold out and I was like, 'What??'."

A month later, things took an even bigger turn for the better. Alan Becker, who worked for the Relativity/Combat/Important group in New York, requested three thousand copies of 'Scum'.

"That really transformed things because I was suddenly exporting three thousand records to a proper distributor instead of posting 20 records to little mail orders," says Dig. "So then Napalm Death took on a life of their own, especially when John Peel picked up on them."

By the time that Napalm's second album, 'From Enslavement To Obliteration', was released in 1988, the furore around both band and label was reaching fever pitch.

"It was definitely strange for us," remembers bassist Shane Embury. "John Peel championed the band as he did a lot of bands from many different genres and helped us get across to crowds or scenes of people who would probably never normally have been exposed to us. The whole grindcore thing was beginning to take over, the indie newspapers were starting to freak out over it all, and then the BBC started picking up on it. Some of my more mainstream metal friends were, like: 'What the hell's going on?'"

Such thoughts were echoed by artists in the more mainstream worlds, and rarely was this intended as complimentary in any way. Rick Astley blamed and blasted the band after his appearance at ▶

Picture by Jenny Platts

Dig setting Slayer alight

Dig with Heresy on tour

Picture by Darren Ciolli-Leach (Baz)

Napalm Death

Dig with Chaos UK and Andy Larsen

Middie, Pek and Mandy

the UK Brit Awards was curtailed, while Def Leppard singer Joe Elliott went on record as saying: "We wanted to be the biggest band in the world and you don't do that by sounding like Napalm Death". Even when the BBC broadcast a programme featuring both Napalm Death and Slayer, the host, Elvira, hardly flattered the band by describing them as akin to have your brain liquidised.

"They weren't impressed!" laughs Mick Harris. "[But] it wasn't something that we were looking for. Def Leppard had a moan and Dig used one of the quotes on one of our records! That was great that we were getting under their skin!"

"A lot of people couldn't grasp it or understand it," says Shane Embury. "My old metal friends from back home were just about grasping Metallica at the time, but to me it was a natural extension because when I got into music I was always looking for the fastest

"GRINDCORE WAS BEGINNING TO TAKE OVER."

things that I could find and to me this was a natural stepping stone. But not everybody wants to take that kind of route, you know? I remember seeing Sonic Youth on The South Bank Show and people were freaking out about. But I thought that it was amazing, a recognition of something different."

One person who picked up on this new world was Dan Tobin. Later to become a press officer at Peaceville and then Earache, Dan was at the time living in London, a fan of metal and rock music in general, when one fateful night he was to encounter Napalm Death.

"I distinctly remember being in the kitchen at my girlfriend's one evening and the radio was on," he recalls. "There was this racket coming out of it, and I was thinking: 'What the hell was that?' It was amazing. My girlfriend thought it was dreadful! I went into a record shop the next day, and said to the guy that I didn't know what it was, but there was this racket on the radio last night, and he just went: 'Napalm Death' and I came away with 'From Enslavement…'. I was flummoxed but intrigued by it at the same time, and that started my love of Earache. I didn't leave things behind; I was still a fan of Def Leppard, but it opened my eyes to other things."

Slowly but surely, releases on Earache were beginning to find attention in scenes outside of hardcore and metal audiences. Napalm Death had supported the likes of Killdozer and Naked Raygun in 1988, Godflesh were the band that non-Earache fans could get behind (with everyone from Danzig to Metallica name-checking them in interviews), and there was a certain amount of unity in the wave of noisy guitar bands vomiting forth from the sewers of the British underground. The world of 'UK noise' was notably captured by the 'Pathological' compilation, put together by Kevin Martin (then of God, now best known as The Bug), an album that was marketed by Earache after Martin ran into financial difficulties. ♠

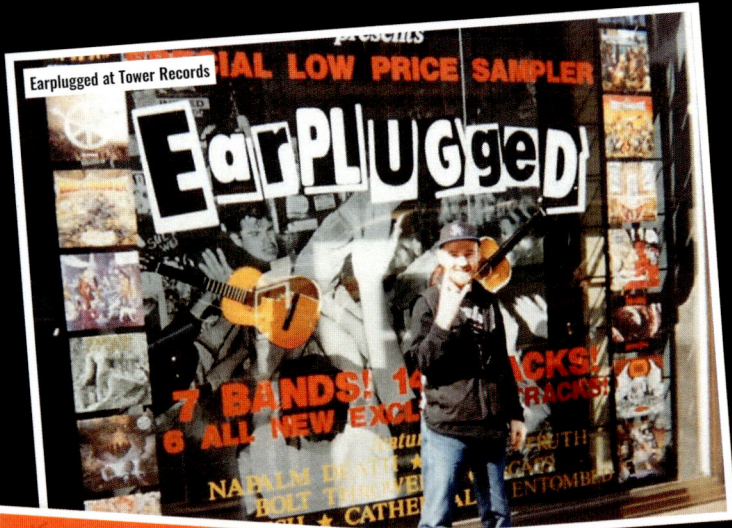

Earplugged at Tower Records

EarPLUGGED

...IAL LOW PRICE SAMPLER

7 BANDS! 14...CKS!
6 ALL NEW EXCL...

NAPALM DEATH ★...
BOLT THRO...AL...ENTOMBED
...CATHED...

Rock City

No. / No. / No.

8 TALBOT STREET, NOTTINGHAM
Tel. 0602 412544

TUE. 14th NOV. 1989 / TUE. 14th NOV. 1989

J.L.P and Earache Records present
Tuesday, 14th November, 1989
8pm—2am
A THRASH EXTRAVAGANZA

NAPALM DEATH

Special guests — MORBID ANGEL — CARCASS —
BOLTHROWER

Tickets £5.50 in adv.   Door £6.

NAPALM DEATH / NAPALM DEATH

MUST BE 18 YEARS AND OVER
PROOF OF AGE MAY BE REQUIRED

Tickets £5.50 adv. / Tickets £5.50 adv.

THE MANAGEMENT RESERVE THE RIGHT TO REFUSE ADMISSION
No refunds unless Gig is cancelled

To be given in / To be retained

CHAPTER TWO
EXTREME METAL TAKEOVER

Napalm Death

Earache's status as THE death metal label has, over the years, come to overshadow the breadth of the catalogue that Dig curated before the death metal explosion of the early 1990s. There was the sludgy grunge of Fudge Tunnel, post-Napalm Justin Broadrick was in Sweet Tooth with Dave Cochrane and Scott Kiehl, and Bolt Thrower and Godflesh amply demonstrated just how punishing taking things s-l-o-w could be. There was even a techno record popping up in the shape of Mighty Force.

"I was switched onto that scene because of being involved with the Hunt Saboteurs Association and the gigs that used to go on around [Colchester]," says Paul Ryan, formerly of Cradle Of Filth and Blood Divine. "There was a bunch of stuff around at that time; Doom, Doctor And The Crippens, Napalm, ENT, that were gigging around Ipswich and they used to put on these benefits for the HSA. I had been involved in sabbing when I was younger, so that's primarily what got me into the more extreme end of music.

"Dani [Filth] and I, we were at school together; we were hanging out and doing things band-wise," he continues. "We all kind of knew the same people and it was all linked in with the Hunt Sabs. I think the first gig I went to was Extreme Noise Terror, and that got me switched on to listening to John Peel. He was playing a lot of that stuff and turned me on to it. So I reckon 'FETO' was probably the first one and then from that I got 'Scum', then 'Symphonies Of Sickness' and it snowballed from there. What was interesting at the time was that it was a gateway. Looking back at it, I'm kind of intrigued that at the time we were getting into that stuff, crust punk into the kind of grind thing, people were citing Repulsion and Morbid Angel and that sort of stuff that was kicking off as influences; the pioneers of what became death metal. I feel very privileged that this kind of music didn't exist, we were discovering it for the first time."

"I was the kind of person that was programming my VCR to record 'Headbangers' Ball' on MTV," says Cult Of Luna's Johannes Persson, "and I specifically remember the 'Covenant' video from Morbid Angel; I thought they were coolest band that

Trey Azagthoth

I'd ever seen. It seemed like every good band was on Earache! Then there was a period when I was listening to mostly hardcore, and I remember Earache signing Coalesce. That was like kicking at an open door. 'Slaughter Of The Soul' [by At The Gates, 1995] is, to this day, an album that I never get tired of."

Håvard Ellefsen, later to reinvent himself as Mortiis, adds: "I did like that Mighty Force record ['Dive', 1991]. It was programmed, dance floor stuff, not as dark as GGFH but really good."

While Earache's divergence from the grind and the death would become notorious years later, Mortiis sums up: "You could never accuse Dig of not being daring or experimental, especially during the 1990s," he says, "but everyone just wanted another Entombed album!"

Earache had also dipped a toe in the world of experimental jazz through the release of ▶

"EARACHE WAS THE ONLY LABEL TO RELEASE THE MAGICAL EXTREME UNDERGROUND STUFF."

Napalm Death

'Torture Garden', an album by John Zorn's Naked City issued in 1991. Happy with the results and a huge fan of Napalm Death, Zorn hooked up with Micky Harris for the Painkiller project.

"Earache had just put out the Naked City record, and John Zorn turned up at a Napalm show in Osaka", recalls Mick Harris. "He said he was a fan and wanted to work with me. I used to go to New York often back then to visit Jim Plotkin and Kevin Sharp. In January 1991 I was over there for a week and John booked a studio. He said: 'We just go in, set up and improvise'. I'd never done that before! I'd mentioned that I'd like to work with Bill Laswell. He was also a fan; his bass had Napalm and Entombed stickers on it. John knew him, and gave him a call. He gave me some money to buy some drumsticks and booked a three-hour session at Bill's studio. I was so nervous. There was a quick introduction and I sat behind this green Yamaha drum kit. We had a quick talk, Bill ran the tapes. Three hours later it was recorded and mixed and the next day I was flying back to Birmingham."

Unlike many of the indie labels in Britain at the time, Earache was far from being UK-centric, both in terms of the acts it worked with and actually getting the records out into markets around the globe. This was becoming increasingly significant as both label and roster began to be seen as the go-to brand for extremity across the European continent, the USA and beyond. On occasion, that recognition would come from an unexpected source, such as when John Zorn toured Brazil and South America in 1989. Interviewed in the national media throughout his tour, Zorn made a point of wearing shirts of Napalm Death and Extreme Noise Terror at every opportunity.

"Napalm Death was the first Earache band that I discovered," says Joaquim Ghirotti, a long-time Brazilian fan of the label. "I don't remember exactly how I heard about them. Maybe a piece on Earache was published in an underground comic book and alternative culture magazine called Animal. This was probably around 1990/'91. At that time I was getting deeper into rock

DEAD HEAVY, DEAD EVIL, ..DEATH METAL!

Entombed
Left Hand Path

Available on ALBUM (Mosh 21), CASSETTE (Mosh 21 MC) and CD with 2 bonus tracks (Mosh 21 CD)

TOUR DATES
with CARCASS

June 1st — LIVERPOOL, PLANET-X
2nd — NOTTINGHAM POLYTECHNIC
(with Napalm Death and Godflesh)
3rd — LONDON
4th — NEWCASTLE RIVERSIDE
5th — SHEFFIELD TAKE TWO
6th — LONDON
7th — BIRMINGHAM EDWARDS # 8 BAR
8th — BRADFORD QUEENS HALL
9th — COVENTRY, THE STOKER
10th — EDINBURGH VENUE
11th — WREXHAM, THE MEMORIAL HALL

Dig with Sam Dunn / Banger Films

Joaquim Ghirotti – long-time Earache fan

Trey Azagthoth live

Dlg with The World Keeps Turning artwork

music, I had some punk records because of older friends who introduced me to some bands, and I listened to some '70s metal and rock thanks to my father.

"But when I found out about Napalm I quickly got into thrash, death metal and grindcore," he continues. "The first recording I got was the Peel Sessions. I didn't like it, it was too extreme and everything sounded like the same. I just couldn't understand it. It took six months for me to figure it out. Someone said that when you meet art like this, or horror movies, or horror images, something that is confrontational, people either reject it and flee, or they embrace the weirdness because it's interesting. I embraced Napalm, but it definitely took a while! I jumped from Metallica to Napalm but it felt like an evolution of sorts."

"It goes back to the late 1980s, when I discovered Napalm Death," says Mortiis. "I was 13 and I saw 'From Enslavement…' and it just looked so frantic, with such dark imagery. I bought it and took it home and… for 1988, that music was unbelievable. It's still unbelievable today. It's almost thirty years ago and it fried my brain. Godflesh did the same a couple of years later; musically both those bands were so different to anything I'd ever heard."

Mortiis adds: "The label seemed underground and fresh and new; there might have been an insert promoting other records on the label, like Carcass, Intense Degree, Unseen Terror, and I' started trying to hunt that stuff down. It wasn't easy as I lived in a small town [in Norway], but every record I got, it was like, fuck me, man, this is a whole new world. I came out of the world of German and American thrash metal, your Kreators, your Sodom, Possessed, and this predominately British sound was being taken to strange places!"

Entombed

Morbid Angel

"Myself and some friends bought the Concrete Sox/Heresy split LP, then 'Scum' and Unseen Terror back in 1987 and we immediately became huge fans of those records as much of the label," says Laurent Merle who, after writing his own fanzine went on to form his own label, Listenable. "We used to trade tapes and were eagerly waiting for 'Scum' to be released. There was such anticipation for that album.

"Earache was the only label to release the magical extreme underground stuff that until then was only available through tape trading," Merle adds. "They were and have been visionaries. When I did my fanzine, I always strived to expose killer underground obscure bands who very few people knew about in various metal and hardcore genres, [and] I have tried to keep such policy when starting the label. It's been like a mission. Earache knew [how] to recognise such appeal and quality in different challenging music genres. Every record was unique in terms of music but also production and packaging."

By the summer of 1989, several bands on the label had received John Peel's seal of approval, not only via the ubiquitous Peel Session but also his selecting of 'Reek Of Putrefaction' as his album of the year for The Guardian newspaper. There was a definite sense that Napalm Death were beginning to cross over into the national consciousness.

"WE HAD A REALLY GOOD TIME, AND WE MEANT BUSINESS."

Appearing in the wake of gigs and interviews being filmed by the BBC, being featured on the front covers of the national mainstream music press and even laying waste to children's TV, the 'Mentally Murdered' EP captured a band truly firing on all cylinders. "We went to Slaughterhouse [Studios] because Colin Richardson was there and 'Hear Nothing See Nothing Say Nothing' by Discharge had been done there," explains Mick Harris. "We had four days to do four tracks. Happy days!"

The band toured the length and breadth of Europe with Japanese outfit Sabotage Organized Barbarian in tow. However, as a reciprocal tour of Japan came to a close, stress, internal disagreements over the finances and general dissatisfaction caused by the band's rapid success would lead to vocalist Lee Dorrian and guitarist Bill Steer quitting.

"I remember, on the second day before leaving Japan, I overheard people in a hotel room talking to Lee and Bill," says Mick Harris, "and I couldn't quite work out whether it was: 'Mick's got to go' or: 'Shane's got to go' or: 'We're leaving'. I had to hold that until we got home. The long journey back was difficult with that on my shoulders, not knowing what was going on. ▶

Terrorizer

Dig called the next day after getting home and said that Lee and Bill have left.

"There was a perception that Shane and I were money motivated. For the record, that wasn't true," Harris insists.

"However, we were tired of getting ripped off by promoters who knew that we only wanted £150 plus £10 petrol money to play. They were making a fortune out of us, and it had got to the point where Shane and I were discussing putting the fee up a bit, and Lee was having none of that. Everything came to a head over such things. We were signing on and off the dole and we couldn't make ends meet through gigging; the money paid for van rental and a driver, and maybe some crisps and a can of pop afterwards. Shane and I felt something had to change."

"It would be interesting to see what Bill and Lee would say about it now," Shane Embury muses. "We were all young. I was 19, [and] in different parts of the country. Micky and I were very close. Micky has quite an intense sense of humour, and sometimes when you're young and finding your feet, you're siding with one person one minute and another the next. Looking back, I wonder if there was such a strong enough unity as there is with Napalm Death now, as we're all a lot older.

"Micky often said that, after the next album, he'd join some band from the States," Shane continues. "He was very spontaneous; one minute is was that; six months later he was going to do a band like Killing Joke. Lee and Bill were shocked by that attitude and maybe after Japan their enthusiasm was waning? Perhaps they saw it literally and thought that all Micky wanted to do was be in some big successful band, and so did I. Well, not necessarily, we were just thinking out loud. That's one aspect and Lee was also getting into slower music. For Bill,

"HARMONY CORRUPTION' WAS A TOUGH ALBUM TO MAKE."

Dig and Krusher

Gaz Jennings

Jeff Walker / Carcass

Carcass were beginning to take off and the way we were with each other it was hard to express our feelings; we weren't mature enough to deal with the situations that we would have been 10, 15 or 20 years later."

While such a split undoubtedly caused jitters at the label, both Mick and Shane moved quickly to put together a new line-up, and headed out on the band's biggest UK shows to date. The legendary Grindcrusher tour saw Napalm Death (joined by Morbid Angel, Bolt Thrower and Carcass) lay waste to the UK, culminating in a show at the 3,500 capacity National Ballroom in Kilburn, North London.

"We had a really good time, and we meant business," laughs Morbid Angel bassist/vocalist David Vincent when pressed for memories of the Grindcrusher tour. "We wanted to give people the full-frontal assault that we had been crafting for so many years. I can't speak for the way in which other bands might have done stuff; quite honestly we didn't pay too much attention to how other people did it. We were in our own little bubble and we did things our way. That's how we expressed ourselves and why we got up and did what we did. I liked all of the bands on that tour and we were happy to be part of something so cool and groundbreaking."

As is traditional in the world of independent art, if a band or record label begins to experience some form of success then the knives come out, frequently from the very people that have helped create that same triumph in the first place. Napalm Death ▶

Lawnmower Deth

experienced it upon the release of the 'Harmony Corruption' album which showcased a new, death metal-influenced sound that had actually had quite a traumatic birth in the Floridian studio where the band had elected to record.

"Micky found things that he didn't expect, working with Scott [Burns] and that was a total learning curve," relates Shane Embury. "Hindsight is great 30 years down the line; everyone perceives things in a different way, but 'Harmony Corruption' was a tough album to make.

"Recording in Florida was a lot of fun because I got to hang out with all of my favourite death metal bands and experiencie America for the first time, and things like sunshine, which you don't get much of that time of year in Birmingham!" Shane laughs. "We were huge fans of Floridian death metal from around 1988-1992, and 'Harmony Corruption' was a very successful album. It was one the first albums that Earache used to launch their label in the States; 'Scum' was the one that Europe picked up on, but the first album that America truly got was 'Harmony Corruption' so it was an important album whichever way you look at it."

Earache themselves were finding that such success brought forth the inevitable accusations of selling out. "Scruff from Hellbastard called me a sell-out when I got a fax machine!" laughs Dig. "He was, like: 'What have you got a fax machine for?' And I'm thinking: 'Er… to be able to communicate with people around the world?'"

Lee Dorrian / Cathedral

LG Petrov / Entombed

CHAPTER THREE
ART & CENSORSHIP

The label would be on the receiving end of even less-desired attention in 1991 when its offices were raided by the vice squad. To put everything into context, the underground counter-culture that existed from the mid-1980s to the mid-1990s had the potential to be life-changing in less positive ways. Censorship was becoming a big problem, with seemingly innocent (in today's world) activities, such as purchasing uncertificated horror films or an underground fanzine, had the potential to end in police raids, fines and even a prison sentence.

In the sphere of extreme music, Peaceville had had distribution problems with at least one Autopsy album cover, Cannibal Corpse's sleeves were being censored, and Dismember and their UK distributor found themselves in court, charged with obscenity, over the artwork and lyrics to 'Skin Her Alive'. Such was the climate at the time, then, when Customs & Excise opened up a piece of Earache's mail. Sent by John Zorn, it contained the artwork for the Painkiller album 'Guts Of A Virgin'. With the artwork literally interpreting the title, the label's office was raided one morning. Jon Barry, an Earache employee who had joined in 1990, was the only member of staff that day.

"At the time we were all cramped up in one little office, four people sharing two desks," Barry remembers. "It was lunchtime and I was on the phone to the distributors in Bristol and suddenly the door flew open and all these guys came piling into the office. I was like: 'I'm going to have to call you back'. They said they were the vice squad and were searching the premises. Some artwork had been intercepted on its way from America. Someone had opened it at customs.

"It was a Painkiller record ['Guts Of A Virgin']. The sleeves to those records were fantastic. The central image was an old medical photo, I guess. A woman's body had been cut open and there was a foetus, I suppose it was pretty grim actually. They wanted to see inside the filing cabinets, which I didn't have keys for, so crowbars came out and they were very quickly dismantled.

"They didn't say a lot," he continues. "I told them there was no artwork on the premises because those things came in and were sent straight off to the manufacturers. I don't know what they expected to find but after a while they realised they were probably wasting their time and seemed to calm down a bit. It was only a bunch of young guys surrounded by metal and grindcore records but they were expecting something far seedier."

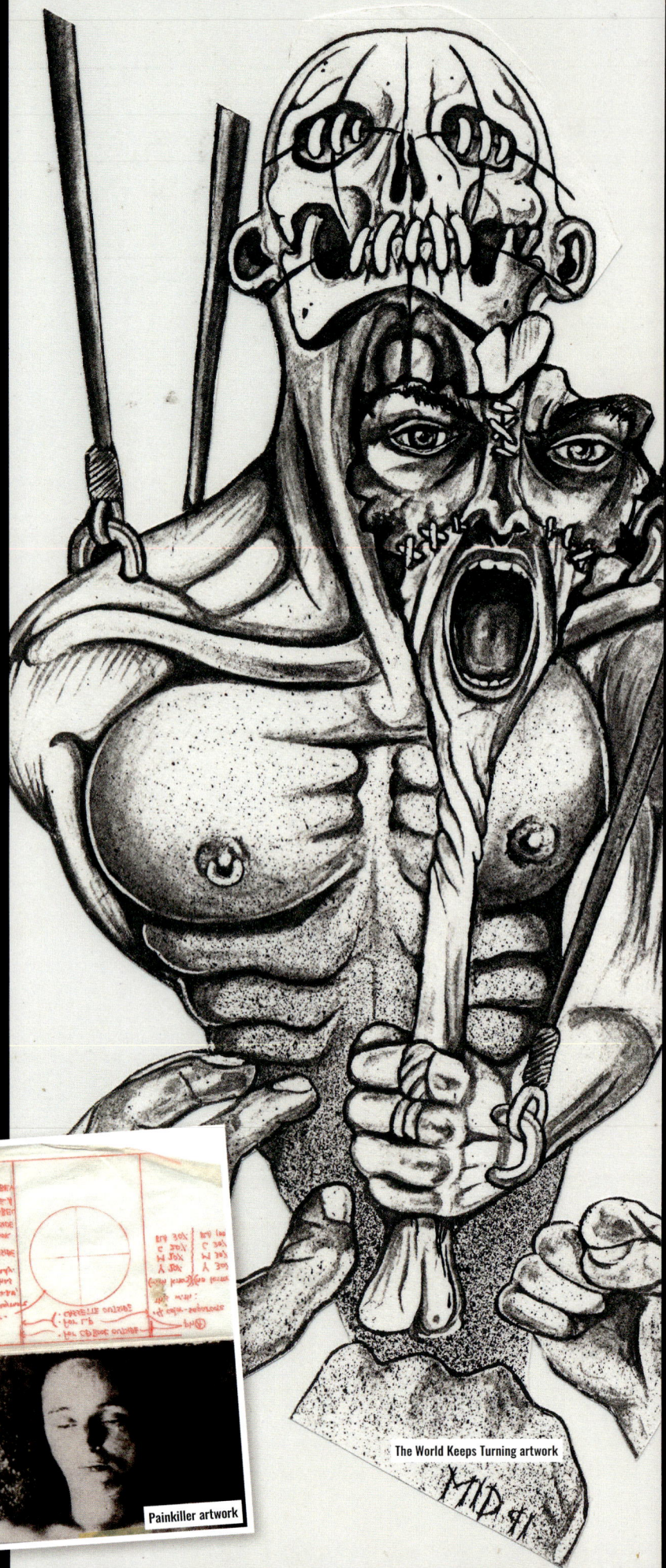

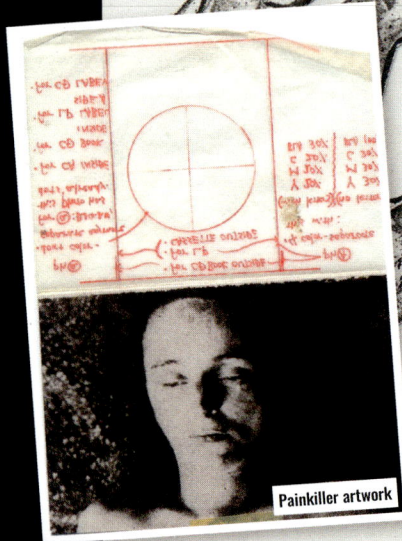

The World Keeps Turning artwork

Painkiller artwork

Mark Sikora and Dan Seagrave

Dig and Matt Vickerstaff

"IT WAS ALL-OUT WARFARE. PEOPLE COULD HAVE LOST EYES."

The police went away with six bin bags full of 'evidence', including, famously, an Alice Cooper poster, and also the proposed artwork for the forthcoming debut album from Fudge Tunnel who were forced to replace the hand-drawn stick drawing of a decapitation from a book entitled 'How To Kill' (which later appeared on a band t-shirt) with something less eye-catching. That wasn't the end of the story, as Dig had to sweat out the possibility of a prosecution which may have ended up in jail time for a full nine months after the event.

Unique for having been an artist signed to Earache – he is perhaps best known as Qualcast 'Koffee Perkulator' Mutilator, the frontman of the thrash metal parody act Lawnmower Deth – Pete Lee was also an employee of the label. Lee joined the company having worked as a singles buyer at the HMV store in Nottingham.

"I knew who Dig was because I always used to see him at hardcore gigs around Nottingham," Pete recalls. "He often came in trying to get me to stock the really early Earache releases. The first one would have been the Terrorizer album 'World Downfall' [1989] and I joined Earache shortly after that. It was a leap of faith maybe, but when you're 18 or 19 we all think we're indestructible don't we?"

What happened over the following five years of Lee's life was "some of the most fun times I've ever had". Pete was taken on as a press officer, but with commendable frankness he admits: "I had no idea what that meant. On my first day I didn't even have a desk – I sat perched on Dig's desk and used his phone to call around the magazines to see if anybody would talk to me. It wasn't too long afterwards that we had to get a bigger office because everyone sat

on each other's knees. Over quite a short period of time things grew exponentially."

Much of Lee's work, he now acknowledges, was "done in the pub or at The Columbia Hotel," he says, referring to the famed rock 'n' roll hangout in London's Bayswater, and times in the company's Nottingham office were "as chaotic as you'd expect for a label that had begun in someone's bedroom and was getting to grips with becoming a fairly large business."

The late 1980s and early 1990s was a strange time in music, and it wasn't always easy to secure coverage for the likes of Morbid Angel, Massacre or Bolt Thrower, though some of Earache's acts such as Cathedral were a little easier to place.

"Those were the days of hair metal and we of course were really swimming against the tide," Lee points out. "But gradually things improved. It helped that just before I joined Napalm Death had got onto the cover of the NME."

The element of fun was always important in the average working day. Pete guffaws: "The amount of objects that flew out of that first floor office window is almost incalculable. We were above a pub owned by Larry Lloyd, the European Cup-winning footballer. Poor old Larry had ▶

to put up with items of all shapes and sizes being launched down below. One day the fucking stereo went out. Mick Harris threw out the microwave. I'm amazed that nobody ever got killed.

"There was a craze when people bought BB guns [air-powered pistols], I think Dig started it," he continues. "Those fights were legendary. They developed into running street battles. It was all-out warfare. People could have lost eyes.

"And then there was an incident involving John Denver…"

Er… John Denver?!

"Yeah, it's true. Our office was directly opposite the backstage of Nottingham's Royal Concert Hall, and John was doing some kind of signing session, so we took potshots at him from across the road. It was ridiculous behaviour, but at the same time lots of stuff still got done – just look at what the label achieved amid bands turning up and lobbing things out of the window, and trying to injure Country and Western singers. It was just bonkers."

Now head honcho of Download Festival, Andy Copping worked at Nottingham Rock City during the 1990s, hanging out on a regular basis with Earache staff and most of the groups mentioned here. During his time there he booked Carcass, Morbid Angel, Fudge Tunnel, Cathedral, Entombed, Bolt Thrower and many more of the label's acts, but one memory remains etched into his mind.

"Napalm Death turned up to play a show and their backstage rider included 3lbs of earth worms – I've no idea why," he laughs. "It was the most bizarre thing ever. Anyway, we sent someone out to an angling store and got these worms, but I never discovered why they wanted them." [Mick Harris had discovered a lifelong love of fishing. – Editor]

"I suspect that's Copping yanking somebody's chain," Barney Greenway responds, somewhat disappointingly. "Personally, I would frown upon cruelty to worms."

We have already touched upon the changing musical taste of Lee Dorrian and its potential role in the formation of his post-Napalm Death act Cathedral. Formed in 1989 to voice an appreciation of slow, doomy, groove-laden yet incredibly heavy metal, their line-up included Carcass roadie-turned bass player Mark Griffiths and guitarist Gaz Jennings, the latter an ex-member of the comedy Thrash metallers Acid Reign, plus drummer Ben Mochrie. Getting their sound right, the band spent the following year cutting a

Pete Lee

set of demos that led them to the door of Earache Records, by then housed in Westminster Buildings in Nottingham's city centre.

"My first memory of Earache was buying Napalm's 'Scum' and the first Carcass album, and here I was signed to the label," Jennings recollects now. "Lee had had a falling out with them in Napalm days but it was Earache that showed the most interest in signing us. Lee had grown up with the likes of Heresy and Concrete Sox who had great association with Dig, and in some ways maybe it felt like the devil we knew."

Back in December 1991 when the band's celebrated debut 'Forest Of Equilibrium' found its way into the racks, the doom scene in Britain was miniscule. Cathedral would do much to remedy this fact, however even the music's beloved progenitors, Black Sabbath, were fooling around with Tony 'The Cat' Martin on vocals, and whilst albums such as 'Headless Cross' and 'Tyr' have their fans, commercially speaking the band was no longer pulling up trees.

"By the time we came along there wasn't even a doom scene at all," Jennings agrees, adding: "In terms of Cathedral's own importance, don't forget that Witchfinder General had existed since 1979 and, like Angel Witch, back then were considered a joke. Now along with Trouble and St Vitus both bands are completely revered which I find very unjust. Cathedral were around for twenty-odd years and I don't think we ever really got recognition for our contribution. We got good press, sure, but maybe we were just a little too strange for the average fan of heavy metal."

Nevertheless, Cathedral captured the public's imagination from the start, with Kerrang! going off the deep end for 'Forest Of Equilibrium' - "this is uneasy listening for the nuclear winter, a nightmare carved in ivory pillars of sound" - before the band went on to become a square peg in a round hole alongside Earache labelmates Carcass, Entombed and Confessor on the following year's quasi-legendary Gods Of Grind tour, and in America with Napalm Death, Carcass and Brutal Truth as part of the Campaign

Bruital Truth

"WE JUST KIND OF WANTED TO TAKE A LEFT TURN AND TRY SOMETHING DIFFERENT."

For Musical Destruction tour.

Though the melodic death meal of Carcass would prove ahead of its time and can now be heard in bands from such acts as In Flames and Arch Enemy, Jennings believes that, of all the Earache acts that might have benefitted the most from the forthcoming cash injection from Columbia Records [see Chapter Five], was Fudge Tunnel.

"Grunge was riding high and they almost had a Nirvana thing about them and they were a super cool band," he says, "but, like us, it didn't happen for them."

Earache's next signing would manage to combine the past, present and future of the label in the shape of New York's Brutal Truth. The past was that the band featured Dan Lilker of noted Thrash entity Nuclear Assault who had long been a champion of the early bands on Earache. Although Nuclear Assault had ended up on a big label, there had been little financial rewards from the pairing.

"People thought Dan was this or that, but when we first started out, we didn't have anything!" laughs Kevin Sharp. "We didn't have a drum kit. We toured the East Coast by hopping on the train and borrowing gear from whoever was on the bill."

Despite such meagre beginnings, Brutal Truth were to pull together 'Extreme Conditions Demand Extreme Responses', an album that while birthed to a very tight schedule and in circumstances of near calamity ("I swear, everything [Colin

Richardson, producer] touched broke," says Kevin. "He would touch the 'Stop' button on the multitrack and it flew off. We were under the gun to get the mix done and he bit into a bagel and his teeth fell out") would, with its mix of Napalm grind, raging hardcore punk and downtempo pummel, catch the zeitgeist of the time by receiving rave reviews from critics and fans alike and also go on to be rated as one of the best Grindcore releases of all time.

Yet Brutal Truth would also be a band to follow the 'Adapt Or Die' mantra. Their sophomore 'Need To Control' album saw the band change their visual and musical landscape, to the point that, despite appealing to record collectors with a multi-sized vinyl box set ("we couldn't find anyone to press a 78!"), the result caused confusion amongst those expecting nothing less than 'Extreme Mk II'. However, as Kevin points out, such an event would have been impossible to achieve.

"We just kind of wanted to take a left turn and try something different. 'Extreme...' became this thing, and we knew we'd never be able to record another album like that, so we thought we'd just try and make a career out of doing different shit. And so we went with this Times New Roman font for the logo and did, like, a piece of artwork for the record which was different from the collage stuff." ♠

Earache staff party

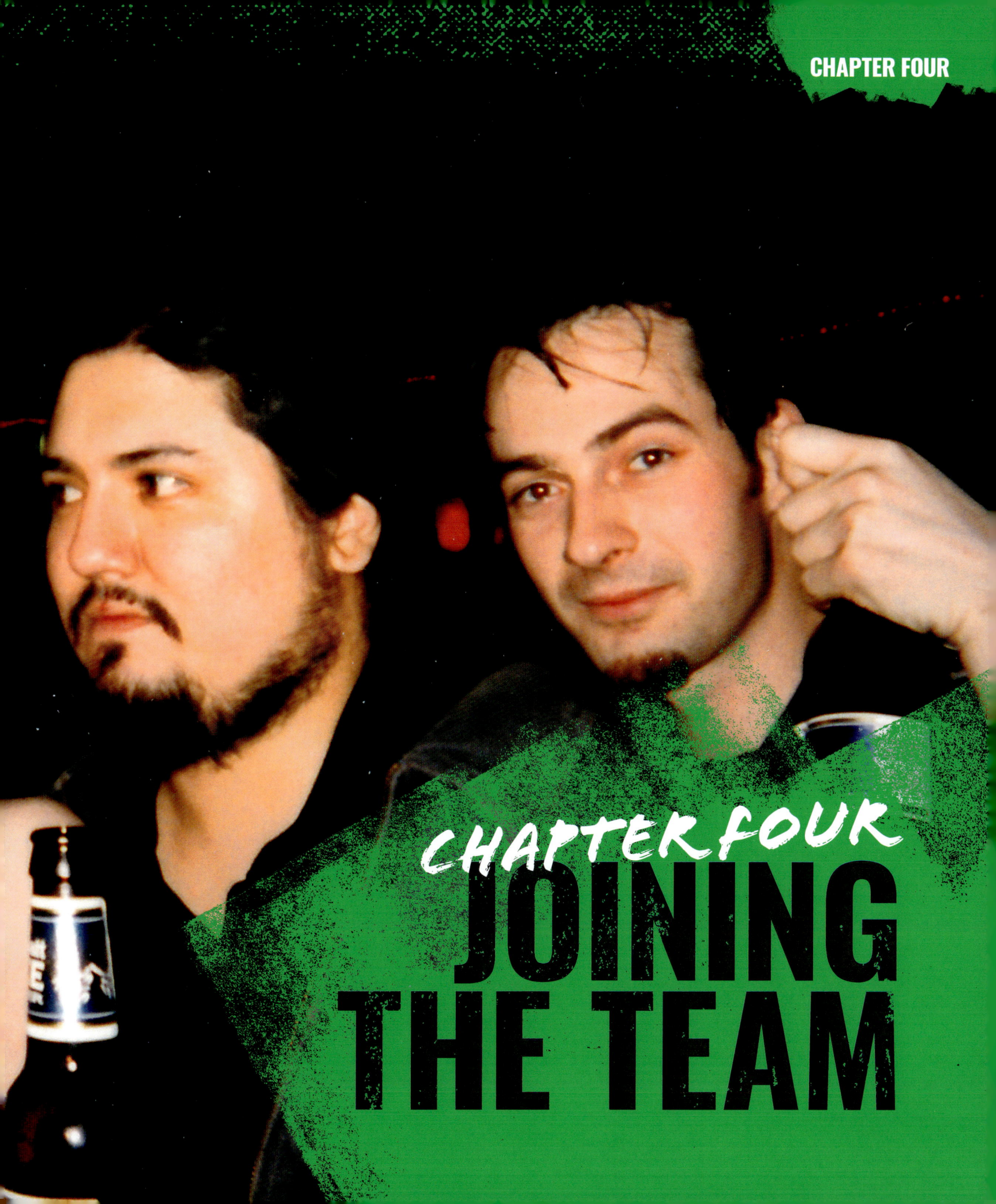

CHAPTER FOUR
JOINING THE TEAM

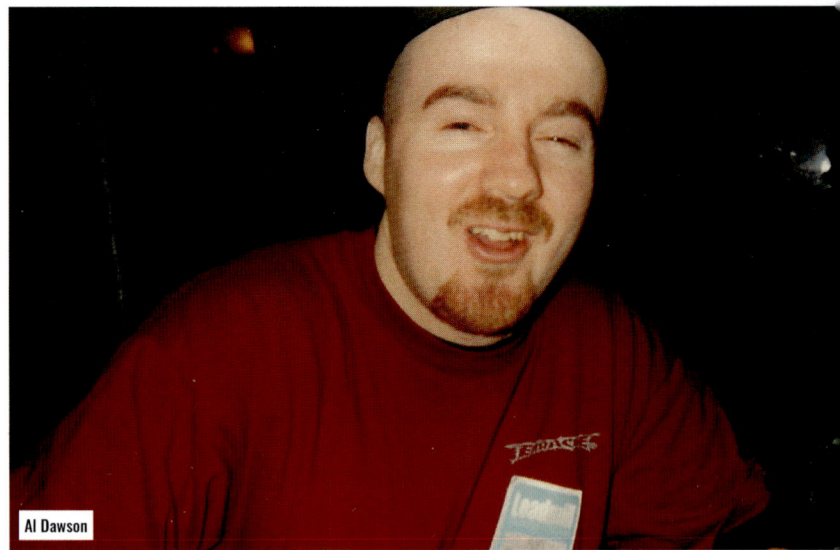
Al Dawson

Al Dawson joined Earache at the end of the 1980s, later helming the label's American office. The Australian expat had first become acquainted with Dig in 1986 through mutual friends. The two were already mixing in similar circles (the 1985 international compilation 'Cleanse The Bacteria' released by Pushead, credits both Al and Dig in the thanks list), and Al, having returned to the UK in 1989 after saving up to make a permanent move from Australia, took up Dig's offer of a job after running out of money while backpacking around Europe.

"In 1986 I took a trip to the UK," he relates. "We stayed in the East End of London, and then with penfriends in Merseyside and then went couch surfing. I ended up staying in Nottingham; my girlfriend at the time was penfriends with John from Concrete Sox and they had a flat in the Victoria Centre. I could only stay a week as someone else was staying the following week and they suggested that I stay with their friend Digby. So I stayed with Dig for four weeks."

Dawson's first encounter with Dig was memorable: "I was drinking with Chaos UK at a pub in Nottingham, and they said; 'Our mate Dig is outside'. Back then, Dig was so straight edge that he wouldn't even walk into a pub; he'd stay outside. Dig didn't start drinking until a couple of years later, and then he'd be necking pints the way you would do when you were a kid!"

Al himself would help to bring on board another long-serving member of the Earache team. Having made the acquaintance of Dan Tobin who, at that point was working as a receptionist for Revolver, Earache's then-distributor in the UK, he was taken with Dan's enthusiasm for the label.

"I'd been at Earache for a couple of years and had gone from being a production assistant to a product manager, doing marketing and that shit," says Al. "I put myself forward for all of the public speaking engagements that Earache had. I used to go down to London and do the sales presentations to Revolver.

"Dan was their new receptionist," he adds. "Back then receptionists were entry point positions, but Dan wanted to be in the music industry and didn't give a shit, so he took the job. I talked to him and thought he was awesome and when I got back to Nottingham I told Dig that we had to hire Dan. Dig didn't get it; all he kept saying was: 'I don't need a receptionist'. Dan was so enthusiastic; I tried to get Dig to create a role from him. And then a couple of weeks later, Hammy [from Peaceville Records] scooped Dan up."

Dan packed up and moved up to Bradford and began working for Peaceville, where his work included handling the fallout from the controversy surrounding the proposed but never finally utilised text on the sleeve for Darkthrone's 'Transylvanian Hunger' album. However, his position at Peaceville was not to last. Hammy had a different distribution model to Dig; whereas Dig would press the records himself and work with different distributors in different territories, Hammy had a full manufacturing and distribution deal with Revolver. When that deal expired in 1994, Hammy hooked up with Music For Nations who bought a share of the label and took over almost the entire label operation. As a result, more or less the entire Peaceville workforce found themselves out of a job.

"So I met Al first and then when Peaceville all went wrong I was going to move back to London and applied for various things," Dan continues. "At one point I was talking to Vanessa Warwick from MTV about doing some stuff with her, but basically I didn't have any clue what to do. I think Al then phoned me at the Peaceville office and said, 'Why don't you drop by Nottingham because there might be an opening?' It turned out that Pete Lee, their press officer, was leaving. So I was interviewed by Al, Dig and Pete Lee, and this was where I met Dig for the first time Dig commented many years later that I was a perfect press officer because I never shut up!"

Peaceville and Earache had been started

> ## "WHEN DEATH METAL EXPLODED IN THE EARLY 1990S, EARACHE FOUND THEMSELVES AT THE CENTRE OF THE STORM."

Dan Tobin / Press Officer

as proper record labels at around the same time; while Dig initially released flexi discs, Hammy had released tapes under the Peaceville banner since the early 1980s. While Earache's profile initially took off in the UK with 'Scum', Peaceville's stock rose higher when Paradise Lost became phenomenally successful across Europe. While simultaneously releasing the likes of Autopsy, Darkthrone, Pentagram and At The Gates, Peaceville became best known for what became known as 'Northern Doom', with Paradise Lost, My Dying Bride and Anathema ruling the roost.

"It was more professional," says Dan on life at Earache following his Peaceville stint. "The bands were bigger and Dig was… [pauses]… Hammy was completely focused on his label, but the operation he had there, the building was horrible, there were rats, I don't remember there being running water, it was freezing cold. In the winter I'd sit there and type with gloves on. I'm not precious about things like that, but come on! At the same time, Hammy was trying to find his way, the same as Dig was doing. There was no corporateness to it. Dig was more focused and more switched on and he was definitely more fanatical in his approach to, a 'wider scope' is the best way to put it. Hammy didn't really seem to care about America that much; Dig was well into that, and the difference was that Peacevillle retained that local scene. My Dying Bride were living up the road, Academy [Studios] nearby, and it was quite a little club really whereas Dig had already got that out of the way by working with bands

like Entombed and Morbid Angel. There was definitely a bigger focus."

When death metal exploded in the early 1990s, Earache found themselves at the centre of the storm, with numerous albums on the catalogue now seen as the definitive recordings of the genre. As had already been proven, despite opinions to the contrary, the label was not hell-bent upon tying itself down to one particular genre and while their existing roster rode the wave, Earache was also sniffing around the nascent second wave of black metal that was beginning to make an impression. Its exponents has begun by bad-mouthing death metal and, in order to back up those words with actions, commenced upon a series of church burnings and other activities that went far beyond anything that had come before. Earache, now infamously, invited one of the key players over to Nottingham to discuss a possible record deal.

"We had a Norwegian early Death Metal band called Cadaver with a guitarist named Anders [Odden] who I became really friendly with," Al explains. "At the time Norway really wasn't on the map musically. We'd talk once a week, and sure enough when black metal started to break, all of those people were looking up to Anders because he was literally the first extreme metal band that had an overseas record deal, so from the very early days we were in touch with the whole Norwegian scene."

Those conversations between Earache and Odden led to an introduction to Varg Vikernes, also known as Count Grishnackh from Burzum. Although some time would pass before Vikernes ▶

was convicted of arson and the murder of his rival Euronymous, eventually serving 14 years in prison, his name was already becoming infamous since Kerrang! had interrupted its steady rotation of Bon Jovi, Metallica and Guns N' Roses to make him a controversial choice of cover star.

"When Kerrang! did that it was such a curveball," remembers Dawson, adding: "Honestly, at that time he seemed interesting to us, so Dig said: 'Let's fly him out here for a meeting'."

A shock was in store when a taxi deposited Vikernes outside of the Earache office, which overlooked the main street. It was Al Dawson who saw him first.

"The guy was wearing full Viking chainmail, like something from 1300 AD," he laughs, recalling the spectacle. "That shit probably weighed more than he did. We took him to lunch at some upper class pizza restaurant. Dig and I were drinking pint after pint. Vikernes had a pizza and ate it with a knife and fork, and casually starts talking about the Aryan super-race, which was an unexpected topic to say the least. Dig told Varg that he liked his music but that he sounded like a bit of a racist, and Varg replied: 'Anyone who doesn't agree with me is an idiot!'

"We had bands like Napalm Death on the label, and quickly realised Varg's views were too obnoxious for us to deal with," Dawson reasons. "After he flew home we broke off all contact."

"Back in the office Pete [Lee], somebody who always liked a laugh, stands up and says that he'll walk out on the spot if we signed anyone that was into burning churches," Al says. "Wow. Where did that come from? We went down to London a couple of nights later and Mörat from Kerrang! said that if we were signing church burners then Kerrang! was done with Earache Records. Varg seemed too hot to handle. I told Dig that I'd known kids like that in Australia and mark my words, in six months' time, he would be in prison. He seemed that out of control. Sure enough, Varg murdered Euronymous later that year."

Though the act made Grishnackh infamous, Pete Lee remains relieved that Earache steered clear of Burzum.

"To a degree, we were looking at the Norwegian thing with

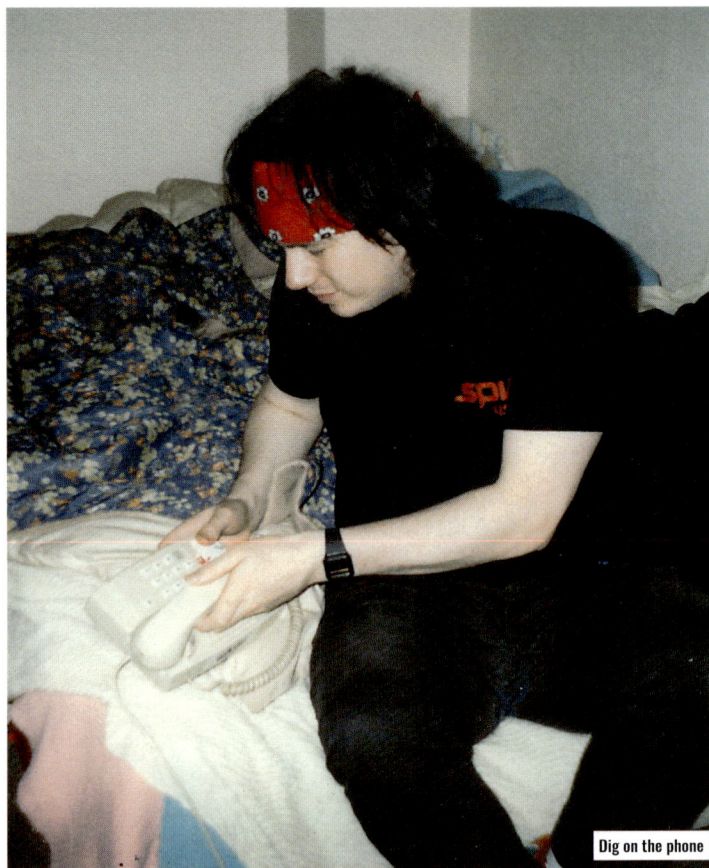

Dig on the phone

Al with Neil Fallon (Clutch)

a sense of humour as much as anything, especially at the start," he says now, "but the whole thing made everyone in the office pretty uncomfortable, particularly when a lot of us came from a punk background. It just didn't seem to sit right at all."

Dig and Al would watch Black Metal rise in popularity and during the mid-1990s attempted to sign both Emperor and Cradle Of Filth. Emperor had not long been reunited after Samoth had been released from prison following his conviction for his part in the wave of church burnings, and Cradle Of Filth were searching for a new deal having parted ways with Cacophonous after their debut album.

"Around 1996 we flew Emperor out and brought Cradle Of Filth up to Nottingham," recalls Al. "Cradle asked for £50,000 to sign plus some other things, as did Emperor. We thought that was too expensive at the time; we'd be paying less for a Morbid Angel or Napalm Death album, but those bands ended up selling up much

> ## "COINCIDING WITH THE RISE OF DEATH METAL CAME THE SURPRISE, STEAMROLLER AND MASSIVE SUCCESS OF NIRVANA."

Record warehouse

Dan Tobin

more than Obituary, Morbid Angel and Napalm Death. Sure, now, it would've been a steal but we just didn't know. To this day it amazes me that bands like Behemoth are so successful."

Another in the long list of bands in which Earache became interested in long before anyone else was Clutch, who had come to the label's attention when the band was recommended to Al and Dig by colleagues in the US office.

"We took a road trip to Philadelphia," remembers Al, "[and] the venue was in a basement right next to a whorehouse – all these hookers hanging out of the windows shouting at us to come on up. We enjoyed the show and took them out to dinner; they were like 17 or 18 at the time. At the end I saw them going through their pockets counting out pennies. They didn't realise that we were paying. The bill was like $45 for seven people; ridiculously cheap. That was a sign of how green they were. They were also asking us questions like: 'What does a producer do?'

"So we pitched a four-album deal with them," he continues. "By law, due to their age, they had to get the deal reviewed by a music lawyer. This was right after grunge had exploded. The majors realised that indie labels were a nice little talent pool for them; Sub Pop had been raided and pillaged. Their lawyer offered to become the band's manager and get them a major label deal, which was a little bit naughty. He walked them into Atlantic and became their manager.

"Of course we were really pissed off, so as compensation the band gave us [the rights to] their first EP ['Passive Restraints',

re-released by Earache as 'Impetus'] which we kept in print for years. We then had to account to Atlantic for sales of the record. Over the years, Clutch have had new managers come in and assume that we haven't paid them, when the reality is that we've always accounted directly to Atlantic and we remain friends with the band to this day."

Coinciding with the rise of death metal came the surprise, steamroller and massive success of Nirvana. In point of fact, Dig had been a huge fan of the band's 1989 debut 'Bleach', to the point where he had offered Sub Pop the (then) eye-watering sum of $13,000 to licence Nirvana's second full-length record – the album that became 'Nevermind' – from them. Of course, as everyone knows, Nirvana's contract was bought out by Geffen and this proposed deal never got past the starting gate.

In any event, Nirvana's insanely rapid success caused extreme guitar music to make an instant appearance on the radar of the major labels. For many years, one particular modus operandi was for the majors to effectively nurture and develop an indie band and, when that band seemed poised to move up another level, make their move to pursue bigger things. ♠

Bolt Thrower

Bill Steer / Carcass

MAJOR LABEL SELL-OUT

Sleep

This had already happened with varying levels of success, but such was the atmosphere of the time, 'the next big thing' could have come from anywhere, and bands as unique and hitherto relatively commercially unsuccessful as Melvins, Tad, Helmet and Cop Shoot Cop were all snapped up. Given Earache's strong sales in the American market, it was only a matter of time before the majors came calling. Somewhat uniquely for the time, Columbia agreed to take on a number of Earache's key acts; standard practice at the time was for a major to pick up bands on an individual basis. Such was Earache's standing and the furore around their releases that the likes of Carcass and Entombed were managing to hit sales just shy of a hundred thousand copies Stateside on what was effectively a minimal advertising campaign aimed at independent record stores and bigger fanzines.

"Columbia looked at it as, Metallica are on Elektra and are selling millions," says Al Dawson, "we don't have anyone like that and we don't understand what these guys from Nottingham

"THEY SIGN TO LONDON AND TURN IN AN HOUR-LONG RIFF."

are doing, but if we throw our million-dollar marketing budgets at their bands, we will have the new Metallica on our hands. So they did a deal to finance our bands and to develop them. Dig did it to move Earache up to the next level. Morbid Angel manager Gunter Ford did not agree to the deal and scored his own deal for them.

"The idea was to take bands to the next level. Carcass signed directly to Columbia," Dawson rues. "We'd loved to have had them on Earache but there were no issues with us when they did. As soon as they signed, Columbia's A&R department insisted: 'Right. You, get singing lessons. We're going to bring in a fashion designer, and make you all wear certain outfits'. Carcass refused, and basically under all the stress with Columbia, the band split up. Columbia called us and asked how much money we would pay to take them back, and then sold the Swansong album back to us."

Upon its release, 'Swansong' was seen as a disappointing epitaph for Carcass who had, by then, called it a day. In a familiar story of Earache releasing records that only really caught on many years after the fact, Carcass' last album for Earache actually went

Carcass

90s Earache team

onto do rather well. This was a story that was to be repeated many times over the years, with records from At The Gates, Sleep, and Cult Of Luna becoming continued sellers long after their original release, as did another album by an early Earache signing who went on to record for a major, with perhaps even less success than Carcass.

"I remember in March 2000 we had a back room full of stock and had 8,000 copies of 'Swansong'," says Al. "A year later, it had sold. All of a sudden, a new generation of metal-core kids got into them and we kept their records in print and alive in retail. But that's the way the music industry works.

"Sleep are another great example," he adds. "They did 25,000 copies at the time but they believed their own hype. Their manager at the time kept saying that we had to let the band go, but they had a four album deal with us. Try honouring your commitments! In the end, they were the first band that Dig let go and they signed to London and in return they signed away their royalties to 'Holy Mountain' in lieu of [monies from their next records]. Sure enough, they sign to London and turn in an hour-long riff. All the A&R guys wanted to know where the radio hit was!" he laughs. "If they had been on Earache, we'd have no problem with that, but London had paid so much for them they wanted their hit."

"There is a funny story about 'Swansong'", adds Dan. "Being Earache we were always into doing some cool formats and new cool collector stuff. So for that album we did a 'brain shaped CD' format. Great in theory and the finished thing looked cool as shit. Anyway we excitedly got the stock in and placed the first one in the CD player to check it played ok. It was then that we discovered a track was missing off the end of the album. Of course being a shaped CD, you lose part of the disc itself and therefore there is less space fit music on. The last track on the album wasn't there! The production manager at the time was called in and Dig went crazy – he'd just manufactured

Massacre

Morbid Angel slime packs

10,000 or whatever it was faulty CDs that were also going to be embarrassing to explain to the band. In fact, Dig was so mad that he sent the production guy home in disgrace. That's why the 'Swansong' brain shape CD has a bonus disc with it, because the bonus disc contains the missing track plus a couple of others to make it look like a proper bonus CD when all it really was, was an attempt to cover up the initial mistake. It must have cost a fortune and is probably one of the worst pressing mistakes I can remember."

On the subject of production mistakes, another infamous manufacturing error springs rapidly to mind, in the form of the limited-edition 'slime packs' that were manufactured for Morbid Angel's 'Domination' album where, possibly due to the quantity ordered, the 'slime' delivered was a totally different substance to that originally agreed on, being as toxic and as dangerous as anything you might find in a horror film.

"As the lead video from the album was 'Where the Slime Live' we decided to do a 'slime pack'," says Dan "[The packs] were coming from the US where they were manufactured, [and] we got a query from the people handling the delivery in the UK. The question was something like: 'What the hell is in this package we've just taken delivery of?' Of course we had no idea what they were talking about and naively asked: 'Is there a problem?'

"There was a big problem. The package had split open and a green 'toxic' material was oozing out everywhere; it had burned a hole in someone's jumper! We arranged a van to collect all this stuff and bring it to the office. We open up the back door of the van and it's like a scene from Ghostbusters; green, oozing ectoplasm everywhere. A few intact samples were gingerly fished out of the debris, and we considered what to do next.

"We had a window cleaner at the time, a right mad bastard called Hendrix. He was the kind of guy that would know how to deal with unorthodox problems, problems like getting rid of a van full of toxic green ooze.

"Hendrix said that he would deal with it no questions asked. We paid him 50 quid or whatever. Years later we saw him in the pub and asked: 'Whatever happened to those slime packs?' He smiled and replied: 'Oh, I just dumped them somewhere!'"

Such incidents presented light relief from the stresses and strains of daily life in the office as the deal with Columbia began to turn sour. Eventually cancelled two years into an intended four-year liaison, the hindsight view is that a combination of Columbia's unfocused promotional excesses alongside the short-termist and myopic attitude of some of the bands' managers of the time both played a major part in ensuring that defeat was ▶

"GREEN 'TOXIC' MATERIAL WAS OOZING OUT EVERYWHERE; IT HAD BURNED A HOLE IN SOMEONE'S JUMPER."

snatched from the jaws of victory.

Al Dawson foresaw problems when he realised at first-hand how cumbersome the operations at a major label could be. They also thought that throwing money at the same tactics used by Earache would provide an exponential sales boost, but ended up simply promoting albums such as 'Heartwork' to the same audience and achieving, more or less, the same sales figures.

"We'd go to these meetings in New York to promote Earache artists and I recall standing in a hallway waiting for a meeting, and some guy was going around with a box of CDs handing one out to everybody. I got one even though I didn't work there," says Al. "Their job was just to work the building. You had to work the building before you could work the streets. There'd be times when you'd meet for lunch, and the time and meeting place would change every five minutes, and you'd think: 'It takes an hour just to go to lunch'! With Carcass, they did 'Heartwork' as the last contractual album on Earache, and I believe they spent a fortune, anything up to a million dollars on promotion, and it sold like 5,000 more than Earache. It was still just selling to the core audience. That was a really hard lesson."

While it is frequently name-checked as their best album, at the time of its release 'Heartwork' wasn't immediately embraced by the band's fanbase. While the songwriting was incredibly strong, the increased utilisation of melody and a more focused and polished sound would have many scratching their heads, at least initially. Bill Steer would reminisce at being told Carcass had 'sold out' by fans while on tour; not least because the band who had pretty much been the definition of gore in extreme metal had utilised an abstract HR Giger sculpture, 'Life Support 1983' as the artwork. Now, a human spine in front of the universal symbol for peace is nothing if not unsettling, but it was far removed from the splatter days of old.

"It was definitely a left-turn in terms of our artwork," says Carcass bassist/vocalist Jeff Walker. "When you can't get the records in the shops, it's self-defeating, and we'd already done the gore. It's not selling out; it's just a bit pointless rehashing 'Reek Of Putrefaction's sleeve. So, we had to move on and do our own thing, which we were doing with the music for 'Heartwork' as well.

"So we got in touch and it just so happened that HR Giger's assistant was a metalhead and a fan of ours, and it also turned out that Giger's girlfriend was a friend of a woman I knew and so it was one of those things where stars aligned. He ended up cutting us some slack as far as the payment went; I know his manager

> ## "NEARLY EVERY MANAGER WAS A NIGHTMARE DURING THE COLUMBIA DEAL, IT WAS WAR ALL OF THE TIME."

Godflesh

wasn't very happy about the fee that we paid! It was £1000, which was still a lot of money for a band like us.

"It was originally going to be a photo of the original sculpture, but he was re-casting it for an exhibition, and he asked if we wanted to use the new version; it looked really good and so he sent us a slide. Our deal with Earache was that we supplied the finished recording and artwork, so they didn't get involved. I think the whole package was a step away and a step beyond what we had done before."

COLUMBIA/EARACHE RECORDS
requests
The Honour of Your Presence at
The Debut Listening Party For
A New Album By
CARCASS
"Heartwork"

Experience "Heartwork" for the first time while enjoying a private viewing of the works of H.R. Giger at

Alexander Gallery
980 Madison Avenue 3rd Floor
(77th St. and Madison Avenue)

November 5, 1993
6:30 - 8:30 PM
Food and drink will be served

Carcass will be in attendance. The band will be performing the following evening, November 6, at 9:30 PM at the Limelight.

Directions By Train - From the CMJ convention at the Waldorf Astoria, take the 6 train at 51st and Lexington and get off at 77th and Lexington. Gallery is 2 blocks west of Lexington.

RSVP 833-5022

HR Giger/Heartwork launch

Compounding the problems were that, with the exception of Morbid Angel, the bands who were now playing in the major label world lacked the sort of managerial muscle that could actually help move things forwards. Instead of taking a pragmatic approach and perhaps playing to the strengths of the deal, many of the managers involved simply saw the deal with Columbia as winning the lottery, the chance to make their mark, a way of getting out of the deals with Earache or a combination of those things.

"The managers at the time, my god!" exclaims Dan Tobin. "You wouldn't believe what used to go on with them. I saw Al Dawson's big, heavy oak desk flipped over by a manager in a rage. We went from all being mates together to violence ensuing in the office. You also had managers trying to take bands off the label, most famously with Entombed, who lost momentum. They were at the height of their game. I remember sitting down with Phil Alexander, who was the editor at Kerrang! at the time, saying that with their next album they'd put Entombed on the cover. It would have been huge. Instead, manager man comes in with his briefcase and tells Dig: 'This band is no longer on your label'. They still had one album to go, so they got off after much battling and lost so much momentum that they never really recovered from it."

Close up of H.R. Giger art to show watches

"Nearly every manager was a nightmare during the Columbia deal, it was war all of the time. Columbia were supportive; a lot of people talk shit about Dig but he bent over backwards to try and get everyone to sell as much as they could," says Al. "These new managers thought if you were on a magazine cover, that obviously means you got a million dollars in the bank. We actually had one manager, who didn't believe the

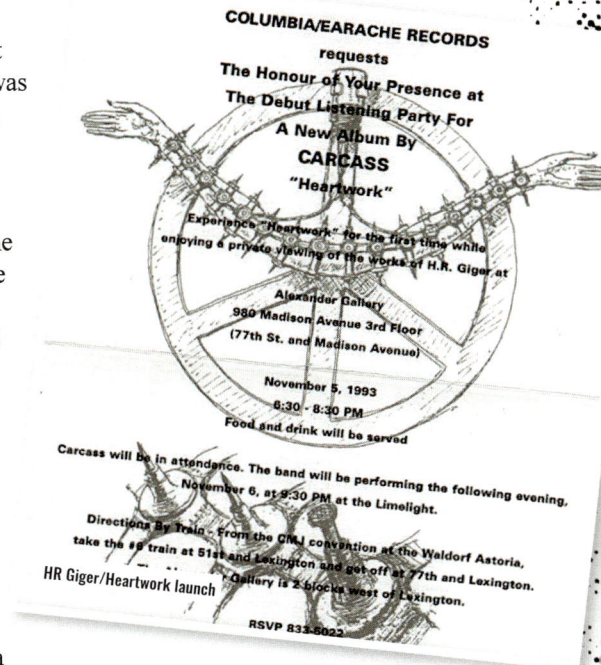

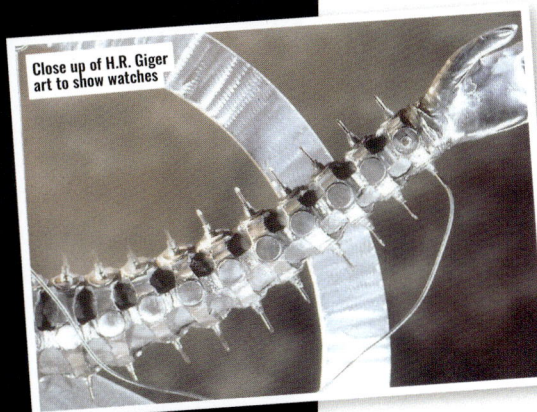

Napalm Death

finances and he did an audit of us. We had investigative financial accountants poring over the books. They found one penny discrepancy after two weeks of intense investigation!"

"The deal was already unravelling when I started at Earache and I was too inexperienced to understand it at the time," Dan continues. "All I remember from that time was total stress and Dig and Al really having a hard time keeping it all together. You had to have a thick skin.

"You can look back and laugh now because there were some people screaming abuse at you and down the phone for half an hour, but at the time it was pretty demoralising," he sighs. "One instance, I was almost reduced to tears. I got such an ear-bashing I actually held the phone away from my ear while the manager was screaming. I hung up on him and he phoned back and went even more mental. I couldn't escape. I had to go to the pub and had the loneliest pint in my life.

> "BUT EVERYONE WAS INSANE, THERE WAS A LOT OF PRESSURE AND A LOT OF MONEY BEING PUMPED INTO THOSE BANDS."

"But everyone was insane; there was a lot of pressure and a lot of money being pumped into those bands. I think Columbia put in a fortune. You only have to look at the videos to see that. I think the accusations at the time that Dig was somehow pocketing the money or that Dig was the only one benefitting from the deal masks the stupidity of some of the people involved. Right now, there are plenty of examples of non-mainstream rock bands doing perfectly well by using the major machine to their own advantage, such as Mastodon. The only manager that had any handle on what he was doing was Gunter Ford. Morbid Angel set themselves up very nicely in America and I don't hear any stories about them falling out with Giant, I think the deal just came to an end."

"Well, we were the only band of our type," says David Vincent on Morbid Angel's situation. "Giant wasn't a metal label, let's put it that way. We were the black sheep. That's fine; we didn't really ask for a lot, but the one thing that they did really help us with was being able to get some proper videos done and being able to get them on MTV and some tours. That was really helpful. Of course, you have to pay back that expense, but we were able to make a video and then that video is also available for Europe so, you know, their quality was so good that thankfully we got a lot of airplay with them."

Al Dawson offers further thoughts on the failure of the Columbia experiment, and why Morbid Angel flourished as a part of their Warner Brothers subsidiary.

"Columbia underestimated the way extreme music worked," he believes. "Gunter sat in on Giant's corporate meetings and

Bolt Thrower

when someone said: 'Morbid will be the next Metallica, we're going to spend $2.5m on marketing and knock it out of the park' he told them to budget accordingly – no way would they sell more than 150,000 copies. The major world is used to people talking in millions and it confused them. Sure enough, they sold that and got their contract renewed for the next album. At the time, we were making videos and the only show in America that would show metal music videos was Beavis & Butt-Head, and Morbid got played on that."

"Carcass were at the top of the game at that point; they could have dominated and what do we get? Bloody 'Swansong'!" rues Dan Tobin. "I like 'Swansong', but after 'Heartwork' they were ready for the big time. They had the attitude, they had the chops and the talent but not the smarts to knuckle down and make it happen. Those deals could have been used to the band's advantage [but were] used to have a moan at the person who has pushed your records for the last few years and has helped get you where you are. Cathedral had a go at it, but didn't really embrace it. Some of the decisions made by bands and managers were not the smartest. I know Dig took it badly, but I can understand that because it's

basically your best friends telling you to fuck off and by the way we've always hated you. That must be a horrible feeling. I had it later myself down the line with bands that I signed."

Al Dawson adds: "Once the Columbia Records deal was done not all the bands were happy with who was going through the major system and who was going to remain on Earache for the USA.

Bolt Thrower came to our office for a big meeting and told us that they were dismayed that they were not hand picked by Columbia, as they were clearly more deserving than say a band like Fudge Tunnel. We had to explain to them quite simply it was not all just about UK and European profile but the fact the A+R guys saw potential in Fudge Tunnel to possibly be a new Nirvana."

"When they saw that they would become a huge priority for our US staff to work and market and not be lost in the major label system, they chilled out for a bit but still their feathers had been ruffled.

"Somehow it kinda all worked out for them since some of the bands that went to Sony pretty much imploded, not being used ▶

Fudge Tunnel

EARACHE

"THE SHIFT TOWARDS TECHNO BROUGHT ABOUT A NEAR-LEGENDARY BACKLASH FROM EARACHE'S FANBASE"

to the way the majors operated versus say a street level Indie label - and it's well worth noting that Bolt Thrower, though currently disbanded, remain legendary in the US metal scene to this day."

"Cathedral kind of semi-played the game," says guitarist Gaz Jennings. "We felt we had to, that we had one chance to be on a major and see how it went. But to be honest we didn't really think we were going to be the next big thing, we realised that early on. 'Soul Sacrifice' for me at the time sounded so good, and when we did 'Ethereal Mirror' we got a big-shot producer but we wanted to sound like that EP! We were all from council estates and a relatively poor background, and for the second record we go to The Manor, this huge studio with a £75,000 budget!"

"The whole Columbia thing was very strange," Jennings muses. "We did a couple of American tours, doing meet and greets and being taken to lavish restaurants, and how much money was being spent was baffling. For bands like Iron Maiden and Metallica it was the norm, but for a band like ourselves… Well, we couldn't get our heads around it. We knew it would turn sour at some point, so we just rode it out."

"Maybe we went too far with the 'disco-doom' thing," he adds. "Without doubt we wore some strange gear, including Lee's white suit. No wonder people were scratching their heads."

"We were an underground band one minute and the next minute Columbia tried to present us as the next Black Crowes," Dorrian said witheringly during the years that followed.

"Dig tried to push as many bands as he could through to Columbia," Tobin reflects. "That wasn't because he wanted to spread his bets, he genuinely thought that all those bands could take off. What happened was the bands that got picked all started fighting with each other, and those left out got the hump and started creating problems.

"When none of those bands broke through, everyone had egg on their face," Tobin admits. "I know Dig's accused of signing bands over to Columbia without their knowledge but I can't believe that there wasn't a whole long discussion process before that happened. You can't do anything in this business secretly. It was done with the right intentions but the bands could have made more of it.

As the dust from the Columbia fallout settled, there was a sense of deflation that seemed to affect both the bands on Earache and the label itself. Carcass had called it a day, Entombed had jumped ship with hearts set on something bigger, Godflesh were becoming increasingly outwardly influenced by dub and the burgeoning drum and bass scene, and David Vincent had parted ways with Morbid Angel to join his (then) wife as a member of Genitorturers.

Morbid Angel

At The Gates

Earache was now about to demonstrate that it knew about extreme metal, which was one of the first times that an established band had joined the label, rather than being signed from scratch. That band, At The Gates, went onto deliver an album ('Slaughter Of The Soul') that's regarded among the jewels of the Earache catalogue crown.

"Hammy had sold Peaceville to Music For Nations and Hammy had always treated us well, but on Music For Nations we kind of got lost amongst all the other big fish," comments Tomas Lindberg, vocalist for At The Gates. "So after 'Terminal Spirit Disease' we did some touring and there were some issues where we felt that the label wasn't supportive enough. Earache approached us at exactly the right moment. We were actually stranded in the UK on a tour, kind of bankrupt in a way, and had to borrow money from another label, Black Mark, to get home. If we couldn't produce the money within a month we had to release the next record on Black Mark. Earache said they could release us from that debt.

Dig got into our demos and signed us! So we were lucky. We don't regret those Peaceville years at all, but moving to Earache at that time of our career was the best thing for us."

"We went back to Studio Fredman to record," Tomas continues, "but basically the legendary story is that we forced [producer] Fredrik Nordström to buy a new mixing console in order for us to record the album there. So he spent his part of the advance buying the equipment we needed and he was refurbishing the studio right before we went in. It felt new, and I think it was the first 'big record' he had worked on, so it was a big step for both him and us."

Unveiled in November 1995, just as death metal was being superseded by several other genres, 'Slaughter…' yielded respectable reviews and reasonable sales figures. The perception is that At The Gates and their album blew up globally and it's certainly true to say that they became increasingly popular, but 'Slaughter…' was a slow-burner that has continued to sell consistently come rain or shine.

Entombed

"It emerged at a time where death metal was standing still a little bit, and other kinds of subgenres were more popular, so we got some decent reviews and it did better than our previous records but it wasn't the explosion that people might think it was nowadays," Tomas agrees. "It definitely did better than our previous records and got us on some bigger tours, but it actually picked up after the band had split up."

In preparation to promote the album, At The Gates were booked on a series of tours that criss-crossed the globe and the end result was a schedule so gruelling that it broke them apart.

"Yeah, we did one UK tour, two European tours and two US tours, and we were scheduled to go to Japan and Australia right when we broke up; a lot of things were going on," Tomas recalls. "We had toured more than we had ever done and one of the reasons that the band folded was because we were not ready, in that sense. We were performing well, and we knew the work we had to put in, but we were very young and touring the world for year straight was mentally hard, and that was something that we hadn't really prepared for."

"I remember clearly being at the [London] LA2 show with Dissection and it was pandemonium – it felt as though the band was going to happen, what I didn't know was that we were going to work them into the ground!" Dan laughs. "That was a real lesson to me: You can't just treat bands like animals. I recently found a schedule for them that I'd created and it was sheer brutality; they ended up hating each other."

After the demise of At The Gates, Earache diversified in a way that it had not done previously. Death metal and grindcore had been the bread and butter of the label for many years, but for the first time, those genres began to take a back seat. Seemingly burned out on the styles of music that had made the label's name, Dig looked for the next wave of extreme acts to move the label forward. A fan of the intensity of brutally hard techno, Dig inked deals with the Industrial Strength label, Ultraviolence, Scanner and Signs Ov Chaos, alongside the more traditional (against the techno, at least) strains of Dub War and Pitch Shifter.

While the label still continued to work with many dominating forces of death metal, the shift towards techno brought about a near-legendary backlash from Earache's fanbase, with cries of 'sell out' and the like not far behind, even if Earache as a label had by this point a long history of releasing material (be it Fudge Tunnel or Godflesh or Sweet Tooth or Painkiller) that didn't neatly fit into the 'metal' genre (and certainly, in the case of Fudge Tunnel, any such categorisation was bitterly fought by the band members themselves).

"We had a period when we did diversify; [the collapse of the Sony deal] was a big blow to the ego and I got deflated," Dig admits. "I guess black metal had taken hold as well, other scenes had stolen the limelight that we'd had in the early 1990s and from my point of view experimenting was the way forward. A band like Dub War I really liked and that was our one main attempt at getting a slightly more commercial band and pushing them to the hilt but it didn't work out."♠

CHAPTER SIX
GABBA GABBA HEY

Mortiis

"IN THE LATE 1990S METAL WAS UNDERGOING RADICAL CHANGES IN STYLES, FROM THE RISE OF BLACK METAL TO THE GROOVE-FUELLED NU-METAL."

"**W**hen we did the hardcore techno stuff, that's when fans really got upset!" Pearson adds. "I really got into hardcore gabba, it seemed an extreme type of music. It blew my mind and to me it was like a new form of extreme music made with computers instead of guitars. The skill involved in programming that sort of aggression was to be commended, and I embraced it but we actually really pissed off the bread and butter Earache fans. I DJ'd at an Earache party in about 1996 and played hardcore techno amongst the metal stuff and Shane Embury chucked a bottle of beer at me. That was my warning! There are purists in every style but I embrace extremity in different things."

"Dig kind of passes it off now, but at the time he genuinely thought that that type of music would become big," comments Dan. "I can't fault him for trying but it was probably the start of the 'Earache backlash'. The idea within the metal community is that you can't deviate from sounding like this or doing it like that. As a press officer, I had a lot of fun with it but even though Lenny Dee and the Industrial Strength label brought some credibility it was a step too far and possibly an example of us getting a little bit complacent. Maybe we had started to think: 'It's got an Earache logo, they'll buy it'.

"At the same time, I didn't mind fucking around with it because it was good to ruffle a few feathers," he laughs. "It wasn't like we'd gone out and put out an Ibiza range; it was still at the extreme end of stuff. I could see the relationship with it, and I suppose metal was going through changes; Fear Factory were big. It got really fragmented at that time, but I think 'a step too far' is probably the best way to describe it!"

Although managing to get itself shot by both sides (in a parallel to Earache's early years much of the hardcore techno scene in Europe was mercilessly underground and DIY, and resented 'big business', as they saw it, jumping in), Earache's flirtation with techno generated press and TV coverage and, at the end of the day, did manage to sell comparatively well, even if dissention was not limited to just Earache's fanbase.

"We did a lot of work; there was TV advertising and it worked out okay," says Al Dawson. "At least in England, somebody would buy a Johnny Violent CD and a Morbid Angel CD at the same time without batting an eyelid, but in Germany and America is it was far more regimented."

Across the Atlantic there was further resistance.

Recalls Dawson: "We flew out there to give a sales presentation

Dig with Lenny Dee

and Eric, the head guy says: 'This is America, it's not going to work and I'm not doing it'. Dig was furious: 'It's my fucking company and you're going to fucking do it!' I had to take him aside and tell him to humour Dig: 'Work it and if it doesn't happen, it's not your fault; you've done your job'. Grudgingly he did that. And at the end of the year he phoned and admitted: 'We need another volume; 'Industrial Fucking Strength' was our best-seller of the year'! So we caught a lot of flak – 'Earache's gone dance' or 'this isn't grindcore', but it sold well anyway."

Among the problems of diversifying in this way was that Earache had a reputation for some of the most vicious, merciless and unrelenting music ever released and, by this time, that reputation was well known throughout the music industry. Thus, when the likes of Scorn started making waves in the dance scene the perception, from the artist at least, was that they were being hampered at best and ignored at worst by the fact that people had an impression of Earache that did not chime with what they themselves were doing.

"It was a nightmare," recalls Mick Harris. "When Scorn's third album, 'Evanescence', came out in '94 it sold 12,000 units. That was nothing compared to Napalm, [but] all of a sudden elements of the press got it. Dig was totally into it but he let me leave Earache because of the frustration. Earache's whole publicity engine just couldn't deal with Scorn. People just couldn't accept it, which I could understand. Dig did try but he couldn't get the right people to push it. We didn't get accepted in the dance and electronica worlds, it obviously didn't get accepted by the metal audience and it just got very, very frustrating. Major respect to the few that did embrace it, but it was just one big struggle, one big depression."

"When I joined the label as Press Officer I was a big Scorn fan," Tobin explains. "But when it came to getting press for Scorn it was hard going. Mick was getting frustrated, too, I think, at ►

Scorn

"FROM A MUSICAL STANDPOINT, WHAT WENT ON OUTSIDE OF OUR BUBBLE WASN'T REALLY A CONCERN TO US."

not getting the recognition he felt they deserved. We hired in specialist dance music pluggers, we gave the band an imprint label called 'Scorn Recordings' and we did lots of remixes as well, I mean we got Andy Weatherall to do stuff which was a huge deal. We had Coil and all those guys doing mixes and white labels going out the door with no Earache logos or anything."

"At the time, Nik Bullen [a founder of Napalm Death] and Mick Harris were big fans of experimental music and had a shortlist of people they wanted to remix them," recalls Unseen Terror's Mitch Dickinson who worked at Earache for a while. "A chap called John Everall, who is sadly no longer with us, knew all those people, like the people in Coil. To get two remixes from them was incredible really; they were always really secretive and didn't really remix for others. I remember, thinking: 'Wow, I'm dealing with Coil!' It was one of the few times I'd ever been star-struck. They'd ask for Carcass albums or something similar. They were really nice people. And they were relatively cheap, especially against the drum and bass remixes I organised for Dub War. We more or less got two for the price of one.

"Those mixes were the cutting edge people of the time," he says. "That was a period with lots of different things going on. Nik and Mick both wondered, at the time, if they were on a different label whether things might be a little bit different. Some people perhaps were not aware of, say, Scorn because it was on Earache. At the same time, it was on Earache but was so radically different from the rest of the roster that, I don't know, one of those quandaries. It was one of those 'trying to sell it to a wider audience' things. The outward audience probably thought: 'Ugh. That's on Earache. Aren't they all noisy metal and stuff?'. 'No, it's totally different give it a try!' Sometimes it worked. Andrew Wetherall was a big fan and 'Evanescence' did well with the dance press. It's an album that has stood the test of time really well."

One of the most bizarre results of this diversification was that Earache essentially started a sub-label to release new death metal bands. Dig suggested Dan start an imprint, Wicked World, specifically focusing on the very type of bands with which Earache had made its name.

"I didn't push for it as far as I remember, but Dig felt that he was out of touch with the death metal scene. He'd grown up with it, signed the best, sold a load of records but his taste had moved on. However, he knew that we still had to have extreme metal bands at the label and that's what he was tapping into - my

knowledge.

Decapitated and Hate Eternal would both find a home on Wicked World before moving onto Earache proper in time. Hate Eternal was the brainchild of Erik Rutan, who had come to many people's attention when he joined Morbid Angel for the 1995 album 'Domination'. Decapitated, on the other hand, were an incredibly young band from Poland who could barely speak any English, but whose abilities and enthusiasm mirrored the bands that had come before them many years previously. Releasing four well-received albums on Earache, the band's story took a tragic turn in October 2007 when drummer Witold 'Vitek' Kiełtyka died from injuries sustained in a crash whilst on tour in Russia.

"It was that accident that led to me making much more of an effort to stay in touch with bands on the road," Tobin confides. "You send these guys out – in this case these very young men – out around the world, covering huge distances and of course you never expect anything like this to happen, but what befell Witold definitely gave me pause for thought. There have been other accidents since, though thankfully not fatal. Enforcer had a bad one on the Airbourne tour, Hate Eternal went through a windscreen, Cauldron had a bad one, too. You never know, so now I always drop bands a line just to check that all is okay out there.

"It pisses me off now when I read claims that Earache mistreated Decapitated," he continues sadly. "Those people weren't there when I signed the band, or at that first show in Derby. They didn't spend hours phoning scratchy Russian numbers trying to get news when the accident happened. Afterwards we organised money for the band, for Vitek's young wife who had had just had his baby. He had proudly shown me a picture of that child only a few months before. I auctioned all I had on the band for the fund for Vitek; test presses, tour shirts, anything I had. It was a devastating event on a human level; forget the music business. Anyone who thinks differently needs to get a grip."

In the late 1990s Metal was undergoing radical changes in styles, from the rise of black metal to the groove-fuelled nu-metal and the increasing influence of Industrial courtesy of the likes of Ministry and Nine Inch Nails, and the fact was not going unnoticed.

Slayer famously began to exhibit influences of more modern types of metal, and Napalm Death also began to adapt and incorporate fresh influences into the sounds of their final trilogy of Earache albums – 'Diatribes', 'Inside The Torn Apart' and 'Words From The Exit Wound' (released between 1996 and '98) ▶

Dig with Eric Lemasters

– although they, like every band who has tried to change at one point or another, hit the problem of trying to keep old fans happy while trying to add new recruits to their fanbase.

"Really old school Napalm fans just couldn't grasp it at all because the production was so much cleaner, you know?" says Shane Embury. "I think even ourselves, we were working with Colin Richardson; he's an awesome producer but he probably wasn't the guy for us at the time. It's a bit of a tricky one to try and define because some will say we were trying to sell out.

"Had Barney been in complete control he'd have probably wanted us to do 'Utopia Banished II'; that's fine and I respect that," continues the bassist, "but the rest of us wanted to try something slower and heavier."

This idea had quite possibly been planted by Meathook Seed, an industrial side project founded by Mitch Harris. Embury appeared on both of the band's albums.

"As bizarre as it sounds, those drum beats inspired by Skinny Puppy and Helmet were interesting to us and we tried to use that and create heavier riffs around it," Shane comments. "A lot of people hate those albums, but there are also those that got into us via the same albums.

"But that's the great thing about sitting here in July 2017. I'll have been in Napalm Death for thirty years, and I can be reflective," he says. "I'm still really proud of those records; the black metal thing was happening so they didn't sell as well, but they paved the way for a return to our roots, enhanced by what we'd learned from making those records."

"I worked on all of those late-period Napalm albums for Earache when the band was making some changes of direction," recalls Dan Tobin. "'Groove grind' I remember some called it, though Earache never did. At the time, with Machine Head and Fear Factory dominating, the pressure was on to stay with the times. Roadrunner were really firing away and having big success with bands that probably owed a lot to the early Earache acts, but had somehow more relevance at that moment. To me, Machine Head was the new Pantera, Fear Factory was an updated, leaner Godflesh. In some ways we would later experience that ourselves, the band Misery Loves Co. was an attempt by us at that modern, fresher sound.

"Anyway, Napalm Death obviously wanted to stay up to date; they had the credibility of being the forefathers, and they were still held in high regard by members of all of those 'Roadrunner-type' acts," Tobin continues. "The problem was that Napalm Death were having to support the likes of Machine Head and Fear Factory, and not the other way around. Playing in front of these crowds and lapping up the 'Machine Head vibe' must have had an influence on Napalm Death. Every song from the newer bands had a monster breakdown riff, a groove part, or a catchy simple riff that caught the crowd's attention."

The scale of this problem became apparent when Earache attempted to premiere the song 'Greed Killing' from the 'Diatribes' album via a promotional night at Rock City in Nottingham. As ever the dance floor had been packed, but to the

Shane Embury / Napalm Death

dismay of the Earache posse (whose number included Shane and possibly Jesse Pintado, the guitarist who sadly died in 2006), no sooner had the deejay announced "the newie from Napalm Death" than it emptied.

"That was so gutting," Dan Tobin sighs. "And once it finished they stuck on [Machine Head's] 'Ten Ton Hammer' or whatever and the place started rocking again."

However, in February 1999 Earache certainly pulled off a monumental coup by procuring Napalm Death a spot on the immensely popular Friday night live TV show TFI Friday.

"That was a pretty weird time because Napalm Death and Earache were in the death throes of their relationship," recalls Dan Tobin. The opportunity presented itself when TFI host Chris Evans had been playing Napalm Death on his Radio 1 breakfast show. Other presenters such as Steve Wright had a history of using the band's music as 'punishment' for contestants on his on-air quizzes, and Tobin "dismissed [this latest example] as another piss-take"

Chris was really thinking about getting a heavy band onto the show. We could hardly believe it because this was just about the biggest, hottest TV programme in Britain at that point."

"To be fair to Evans, he took the plunge by inviting Napalm Death onto his TV show, he really talked the band up and the impact was pretty huge," Tobin smiles. "We stood out so much – I think the other musical guests on the show were Sheryl Crow and Arthur Brown doing 'Fire' – so we were definitely the odd ones out.

"And after the show we went across the road to the pub where Chris and his entourage were holding court behind a little white rope," he laughs. "And again to be fair to the guy, Evans came over and thanked us for getting the band on, and if my memory serves, he even bought a round of drinks."

There was at least one band on the Earache roster that couldn't have cared less about what was going on in the wider musical world, and would have sooner stopped than taken any such suggestions on board. Step forward, Morbid Angel.

"I don't know how to clarify this point too much," says David Vincent. "From a musical standpoint, what went on outside of our bubble wasn't really a concern to us. So, at no time do I remember making a decision, consciously or unconsciously, based on what someone else was doing. Other than the fact than saying from a production standpoint, when you're listening to guitar or drum sounds and seeing which ones I liked, versus something else, that was perhaps the only comparison that we would ever do. Not from a creative standpoint, but maybe from a production standpoint." ♠

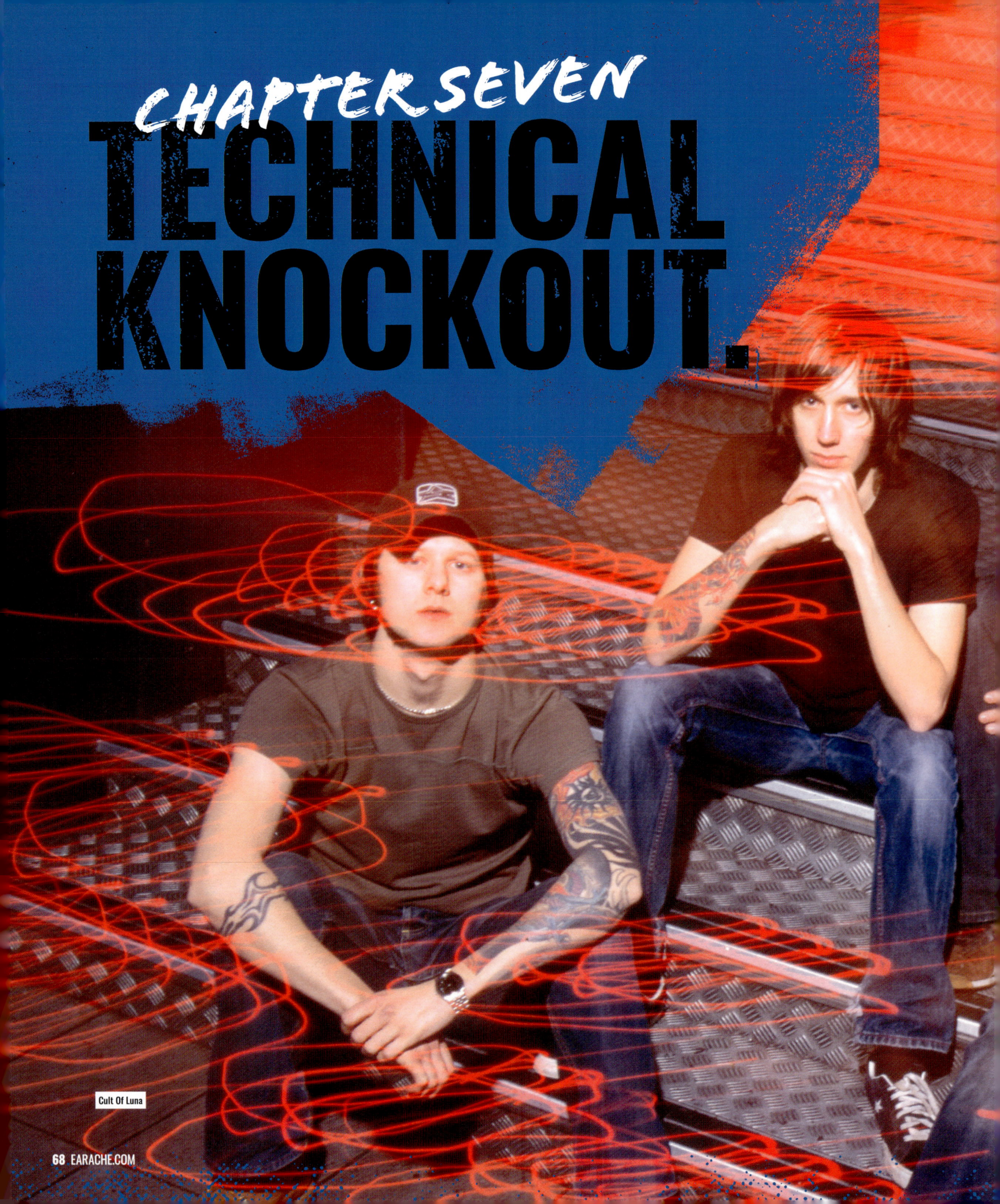

TECHNICAL KNOCKOUT.

Cult Of Luna

Iron Monkey

The times may have been a-changing, but there was still plenty of time for fun, japes and general chaos to find its way into the Earache offices and beyond. Whether it was the office stereo being drop-kicked through a (closed!) window by a pissed-off intern or rigging up a couple of 'phones so that two band managers ended up arguing about who had called the other, or Mitch Dickinson having to live down his inadvertent eating of a meal destined for the boss of Earache's Japanese licensee, it is fair to say that no two days at the office were the same. The same also went for business trips, and stories of alcohol and fireworks abound.

"Dig and I got invited over to Hannover in Germany to sign off the new distribution deal for the territory with a company called SPV Records," relates Tobin about one particularly eventful business trip. "We checked into our hotel, which is in the middle of nowhere – more on that that later – and head to the SPV offices. We do the meeting, agree the deal, handshakes all round, and go for dinner. So far, so normal.

"And then things get weird. We ask about the plans for the evening. According to our hosts, we are going to see the wrestling. I am not a fan of wrestling. As far as I knew neither is Dig. We turn up at some circus tent somewhere and hit the bar. The wrestling starts and we go in to watch; front row seats. I have about four beers lined up in front of me, and suddenly one of the wrestlers tumbles out of the ring and is rolling straight towards my drinks. I react instinctively, and because I have a drink in each hand, I stop the guy rolling into me with my foot. Immediately all around me people are in my face, shouting: 'Don't touch the wrestlers! Don't touch the wrestlers!'. It's totally bad etiquette, but the guy was gonna knock beer everywhere so what was I gonna do? As he climbs back into the ring, I notice he has my footprint on his lower back. The fights go on and on and it's ridiculous. It's not fighting at all; we are so close you can see all the fake punches, the grabs that look violent from far away but up close are just light holds.

"Afterwards, we are taken into the backstage area for yet more drinks. It's at this point that Dig comes up to me and throws a fake punch at me. It's a fake punch of course, and I fake being hit, and he stamps his foot to make the sound of the punch, just as we'd seen the wrestlers doing in the ring minutes before. I [then] feel myself being lifted off the ground, I'm struggling for breath; it feels like I am being strangled. I can't talk, or move, I'm completely trapped.

"Just when I think I'm about to pass out, I'm released and dropped to the floor. I start to recover my senses, just in time to see Dig being physically picked up and then launched down the corridor through the air. There's a huge wrestler dude standing over us, Cannonball Grizzly. He's totally pissed off because he's seen Dig and I disrespectfully mimicking the wrestling tricks we'd seen earlier. One of the other wrestlers Robbie Brookside is, it turns out, a Brit and, amazingly, a Carcass fan. He bundles us out of there, and it transpires that all the wrestlers are pumped up on all kinds of drugs and looking for a fight at the slightest opportunity.

"Anyway, our hotel is located in the middle of nowhere. We decide to have a nightcap and wander into the bar. Guess who the only other people in the bar are? Yep, the wrestlers – all of them. Including Cannonball, who had thrown Dig 20 feet down a corridor just hours earlier and nearly strangled me to death. They look super pissed off. We elect to front it out – we approach

Robbie Brookside

the bar full of apologies and offer to buy them drinks by way of saying sorry.

"They start squaring up like they're going to squash us. The bartender runs around from behind the bar and stands between us and them, and just tells us to run while we have the chance. We run, and I double-lock my hotel room door that night!"

This escapade showed Earache that Metal and wrestling shared a fanbase which the label occasionally tapped into, releasing the official ECW (Extreme Championship Wrestling) compilation album, and later sponsoring Nottingham UFC Fighter Dan "The Outlaw" Hardy, as he fought for the UFC World Championship title.

And if nothing else happened in or out of the office on a particular day, there was always Mick Harris and his love of sending faxes to liven things up. In those days, faxes were delivered on a single roll of paper, so multiple pages would come out on one long stream. ▶

At The Gates

"Occasionally Mick would play a prank and send the same fax five million times or something," Mitch Dickinson laughs. "You'd go in the morning and there'd be one long, Andrex-style, 200 metre roll of fax on the floor!"

The Earache band that took the prizes for A) causing the most offense and B) leaving a trail of destruction and violence in their wake was the aptly named Anal Cunt. The career of Seth Putnam was littered with examples of provoking a reaction for the sake of same, and generally trying to offend everyone in any manner that would get such a reaction, but one of AC's most notorious of incidents was their 1997 UK tour. You would think that not a lot could happen over the course of a tour that lasted for two shows, but no. Dan Tobin had caught the band live in New York, and had

seen an inkling of what might happen.

"I hooked up with some of the US office staff who were going to see AC at a club called ABC No Rio on the Lower East Side. Kevin [Sharp] and Danny [Lilker] from Brutal Truth were there so I hooked up with them, too. I speak to the girl on the door who says: 'Oh, you're from England, one word of advice - stand at the back'. I figured: 'It's okay, I've been to loads of shows and I know what to do'.

"We get in - I stand midway back. The band comes on, they launch into a blur of noise and Seth picks up the mic stand, it's one of those with the plate bases, and he just throws it javelin style into the audience. It hits this guy full in the face, and that's when the expression 'spitting teeth' becomes a reality. I watch a

Sarah with Mortiis

IRON MONKEY HAVE SPLIT UP. YOU DON'T NEED TO KNOW THE REASONS WHY. IT'S NONE OF YOUR FUCKIN' BUSINESS. GET OVER IT.

BUT REMEMBER, WHEN YOU'RE GIVING IT TO YOUR WOMAN AT NIGHT, SHE'S THINKING ABOUT IRON MONKEY. WHEN YOUR DAD IS GIVING IT TO THAT STINKY BITCH YOU KNOW AS MUM, SHE'S THINKING ABOUT IRON MONKEY. AND WHEN YOUR PITIFUL LITTLE BAND TAKES THE STAGE, YOU'RE THINKING ABOUT IRON MONKEY. ALL OF YOU WISHING YOU HAD SOMETHING THAT YOU NEVER WILL.

IRON MONKEY ARE THE PUNK ROCK OUTLAWS. THEY ARE GODS AMONG MEN. SO PLAY THE CD's IN YOUR LITTLE CD PLAYER ONE MORE TIME AND SAVOR THE SWEET, SWEET TASTE OF SOMETHING YOU'LL NEVER HAVE ANY OTHER WAY.   (OVER →)

everyone in to one corner. The wheelie bin goes flying. I'm worrying about the breeze blocks. A girl is at the front of the stage giving him loads of lip, flipping him, giving the finger. He does a lasso move with the mic cord, gets it around her neck, brings her in and punches her in the head. She doesn't shut up though, and keeps on at him through the set. In the dressing room afterwards Seth's hand and knuckles are completely swollen up. Dig takes him to A&E. It turns out the girl had a metal plate in her head and he punched that."

Before the London show, AC had managed to upset a journalist from the NME who was interviewing the band for their 'Dartboard Challenge' section; Seth broke the dartboard, attempted to spear the journalist with the darts and was highly offensive throughout the interview. "I said: 'What did you expect, The Dandy Warhols? The band is called Anal Cunt!'" laughs Dan.

couple of his teeth fall out, then a flap of skin folds down from his forehead quickly followed by what seemed to me to be a lot of blood. The weird thing is, the guy seems to be loving it; he doesn't leave, just continues getting down to the show. I edge slowly to the back of the room..."

Arriving for a later show in Nottingham, Anal Cunt and label staff decamp to a nearby pub, the sort that proffers a multitude of brass instruments that traditionally surround a fireplace with a roaring fire. Seth slings one of the brass trumpets into the roaring fire in the fireplace. Amid much black smoke, the party rapidly move onto Nottingham's Rock City for more drinks and even bigger doses of chaos and violence follow, before the band had played a note. The first show was held at the Victoria Inn, Derby. Shortly before AC took the stage, Seth grabbed a wheelie bin, dumped two breeze blocks and an old door into it, and the band started the show.

"Seth rushes the entire audience with the door, and pins

"They did the show and they were devastating," Dan recalls. "I think the NME sent Steven Wells to review it and he later gave them a glowing review. There were no breeze blocks this time, just ripping grind/noise. Towards the end of the set we spotted police on the top of the stairway and realised it was about last night in Derby. The girl with the metal plate had made a complaint of assault, and the police came down from Derby for Seth.

"So as soon as they finished the set we had to cover him in a couple of hoodies and bundle him out of a side door, down some alleyway and out into the London air. He escaped the law; later we heard they were asking around the venue as it was kicking out: 'Where is the singer? Where's the singer?'"

Another band whose reputation has become legendary many ▶

Mortiis (for The Stargate album)

years after the fact is Iron Monkey. Mitch Dickinson, formerly of Heresy and Unseen Terror, was playing in a band outside of his Earache day job, and became aware of the band in their earliest incarnation.

"Iron Monkey kind of evolved out of pop punk band!" laughs Dickinson. "I was playing in a pop-punk band called Bradworthy and Justin Greaves was on drums. We were rehearsing one day and Jim Rushby was there. We were having a break and he asked if he could play my guitar, and he played what became an Iron Monkey song. He asked if we wanted to jam and maybe start a band, but I chose to stick to one band."

Johnny Morrow was certainly one of the most unique vocalists in extreme music. Quiet and thoughtful off-stage, the moment a microphone was placed in his hand, the unassuming Dr Jekyll would be replaced with a snarling, bug-eyed Mr Hyde who quickly helped to garner the band a formidable live reputation for both his vocal performance and flashes of violence that became the stuff of legend.

"When I met Johnny, I really didn't think that he was going to sound like that," says founding member Steve Watson. "The first time I met him, I had to wait outside the rehearsal studio to let him in. He turned up, and I thought: 'Who's this knob?' He had hair then as well.

"Johnny would… instead of asking someone to turn the lights down, he'd go and break them," laughs Steve. "It was fun to watch, but every gig you'd guarantee that something was going to happen. It made the gigs interesting; a bit of aggro. We didn't know what was going to happen, let alone the audience. We played in Bristol with Acrimony; Johnny threw his mic stand out and the next thing I knew it knocked me out. I came around and

[just] started playing again!"

"Iron Monkey were not well received outside the UK," says Dan Tobin. "I remember being in Germany trying to sell the band to a distributor and they were all laughing at the name Iron Monkey. Germans call the English 'Island Monkeys' like we called them 'Krauts' or whatever – they thought the name was hysterical, deliberately mishearing it. That didn't help. In America there were accusations of Eyehategod cloning, but we got some credibility because the US-made hand-printed Monkey shirts that we gave to the bands there; Machine Head were pictured in Kerrang! wearing that shirt. Then of course Phil Anselmo was rumoured to have OD'd while listening to Iron Monkey. None of this hurt their reputation as bad-asses!"

Iron Monkey's reputation began to take on a life of its own almost as soon as they had ended. Morrow returned to the live scene as a co-vocalist of Murder One, but would sadly pass away in the hours following their debut London show. Since his death, stories of Earache's coldness surrounding this event have circulated, and Dan is keen to put the record straight, pointing out that at no point was the label aware as to the gravity of Johnny's illness until he passed away 2 years after splitting up and leaving the label.

"The common story is that Earache was at war with the band," he clarifies. "What most people don't know is that just a few weeks before he passed away, Johnny came into our offices with live tapes to go through what were supposed to form part of a DVD legacy release we were planning with his blessing. Johnny was co-operating and working fully on that. Just after he left some tapes with us, we got the news that he passed away. It was a ▶

> "IT HITS THIS GUY FULL IN THE FACE, AND THAT'S WHEN THE EXPRESSION 'SPITTING TEETH' BECOMES A REALITY."

Dig and Phil

Arif Rot / Wormrot

Anal Cunt

Dig

total shock to all of us. Only afterwards did it all come about how Johnny had lived with a kidney complaint for all of his life, and how that led to the complications that ended his life."

Craziness aside, one important aspect of Earache's operations has been to give its acts complete artistic freedom. With bigger labels it is common business practise for a company to stamp their mark on a band in order to make the end results more 'commercially acceptable'. Though perceived as the behaviour of major labels, some black metal bands that were (briefly) tied down to these deals have commented that such companies, unaware of what those bands did, allowed them far more trust and freedom in production than the indie labels they went on to work with later in their careers.

"It sounds crazy, but we give bands complete and utter free reign, even to make mistakes!" says Dig. "We do make suggestions a lot, but that's [as far as it goes]. We've only intervened when we think the band are going to make a terrible, critical misstep. But our bands have done missteps all the time; producers that don't suit the band or whatever. Creative freedom seems to be unheard of elsewhere."

"On Earache we were free to do whatever we wanted," confirms Tomas Lindberg. "As I said, Dan was a close friend of the band and we kept him in the loop with what we were doing, but the label never really had any issues. We presented all of the ideas for the cover and the lyrics to them as we went along, but there was never any interference with our creative ideas."

"I never had a problem with [Earache] over that," agrees Mortiis. "They never tried to dictate musical direction, made no demands or anything with artwork or anything like that, or the image of the band. I can imagine that some labels would want to shape those things but Earache never did. I'm sure that had we delivered crap with shitty artwork they would have called us on it, but they had faith that we weren't going to turn in a bunch of bullshit.

"Looking back, I'm sure that [the gothic sound of 'The Smell Of Rain' (2001)] would have come as a bit of a surprise to them," he laughs. "I did warn them that it was going to be different! Actually when I sent in the tapes for 'Smell…' Dig emailed back to say it was a really good album and that he was really excited by it."

"I never had a single 'creative' discussion with Earache," agrees Johannes Persson from Cult Of Luna. "We've always valued our integrity highly, and we've never had the ambition to ever live off our music; we've never cared about that. I've always done what has been expected of me, press and so forth. There was one incident, where for the 'Salvation' album, they put an advert in the middle of the booklet. I can't begin to describe how much that angered us! But it's not a punk label; we were expected to make money. We saw it as pure evil at the time, but they probably did that with every band. It's natural to have conflict with a label; their perspectives will clash; for us it was 100% art, for the label it's at least 50% business." ♠

Johannes Persson/Cult Of Luna

At The Gates

CHAPTER EIGHT

END OF AN EARACHE? ALMOST.

Tomas Lindberg and Dan

Al holding court

Dig at a conference

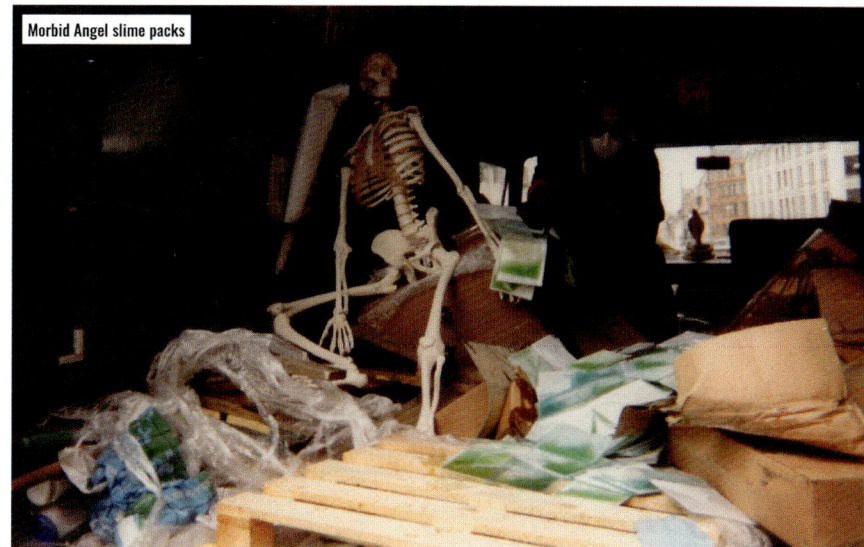

Morbid Angel slime packs

n many respects the biggest and boldest moves on both the parts of Earache and the bands concerned came towards the end of the 1990s, with Napalm Death and Godflesh parting ways with the label; Earache choosing not to renew the respective deals they had with each band.

Napalm Death in particular was the biggest shock as band and label had played a defining role in the success of the other, both initially and throughout the course of the 1990s. What is fair to say, however, that by that time the relationship between Earache and what had once been its flagship act had deteriorated to the point of, if not quite open warfare, then a degree of acrimony that would last for years.

"That was big stuff at the time because we didn't know what we were going to do next," Dan Tobin says. "Napalm, I think, had run their course. We had them for so many albums and I think everyone just got sick of each other. You have to remember that the band was in disarray at the time. Barney left and then came back. Phil Vane was in but it didn't work out, they were trying different styles. Fear Factory and Machine Head were basically eating their lunch and new scenes were coming in, whether that was black metal or female-fronted operatic metal, and Napalm looked a bit out of place."

Nevertheless, bravery was required to part ways with the band that had made the label's name.

"It took guts on both sides," Tobin affirms. "It was pretty acrimonious at the time, but any break like that is unlikely to be smooth. We had to move on, and at the time eyebrows were raised. But looking back it was the right thing to do."

"It [the split] was probably a multitude of things, I suppose," Shane Embury reflects. "I don't want to dwell on it, to be honest, but I can look back from different angles. Yes, from the label's perspective our sales were declining, there was a deal which we were a part of which involved a lot of cash which had been paid to our manager; I think our manager at the time was equally to blame for some of the bullshit as well. I'll just say that it was a massive learning curve for everybody, for us and for Earache as they continued to deal with other bands.

"I was still pretty naïve as to the business side but from what I remember it was a horrible atmosphere," Dan Tobin says. "I believe that, whether the band would agree or not, part of what went down was also due to the frustrations of the changing musical times. It meant that Earache and Napalm Death, and the other big

acts, had to reinvent or reassert themselves to stay with it. All of a sudden everyone was in danger of being seen as yesterday's news – including Earache. It had been such a rapid upwards path to that point and then the first time a couple of records don't sell as well, or a new signing doesn't take off the same way, people start finger pointing."

There was also a similar situation with Morbid Angel. Says Tobin: "Trey had a line-up change after they split with Giant, Steve Tucker came in on vocals; they were treading water on those last couple of records and you can keep on hoping that they're going to rediscover their spark. Ultimately, I think it reinvigorated both Napalm Death and Morbid Angel, and it was a kick up the arse for us."

"Well, we [label and band] grew up together. We had children together," reflects David Vincent. "Regardless of what has or has not happened to either party over the years it's been, in my mind, a very fruitful relationship. There will always be points of contention between an artist and a label, but when I think about our time on Earache and the success that we've achieved together, I'm pleased with it and I'm thankful to Dig for choosing to take a chance on us.

"It took a team [to make it happen]," Vincent adds. "Could some things have been handled better by all parties? Sure. But I think we made the right decisions and it's proven to be a good relationship. I look back on it all with fond memories."

With Earache's key acts either broken up or moving onto pastures new, the label found itself needing to adapt in order to survive. New (and, indeed, nu-) genres were appearing, forcing death metal back underground. This left Earache looking further ▶

"THE LABEL WAS DECIMATED; IT WAS A DARK TIME."

Earache NextGen '98 tour bands

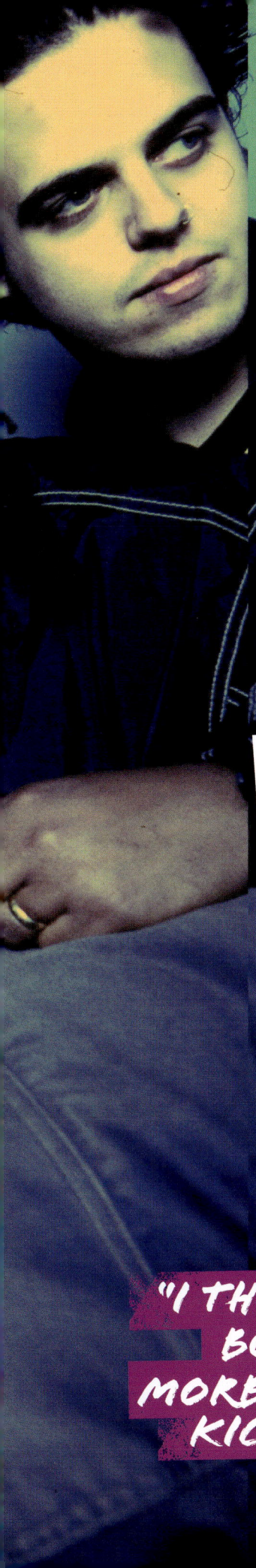

Gizz Butt with Star Wars characters

This is Tobias from REPUGNANT and XYSTER Mag. Thanx for your letter... How are you by the way? I, myself, am fine. Well, what's new with us... We are currently preparing ourselfs to enter the das Boot Studio again now in March, to record our second demotape. Our plans are to record maybe 10 songs (both old & new) in June as meant to be our debut Lp, due to be released in maybe October 2000. Don't know which label yet though, we've been approached by Hammerheart (Holland), but we delayed a signing cuz of our second demo coming up. When our new demo ("Draped in Cerecloth") comes out in March we'll be negotiating with labels for real about a deal. As you probably understand, it would be cool for us to be working with a label such as EARACHE / WICKED WORLD, he he! But I guess oyu weren't interested judging from your letter, but I'll send you our new tape when it's done and we'll see what you think about us then...
About gigs, we've done 3 of 'em so far, with i.e. DISMEMBER, MAZE OF TORMENT and PANDEMONIC. People say we're a good live-act, but I don't know... We're improving though, all the time. By the way, is there any old stuff still available (like shirts stickers,posters/liveposters,whatever) with the old goodies, like NAPALM DEATH, MORBID ANGEL, CARCASS, BOLT THROWER, TERRORIZER, ENTOMBED etc... I'm a collector of practically everything concearning old Death metal underground, either it be albums/tapes or shirts. I'll settle with a torn apart sticker! Maybe some old NECROSIS REC. stuff???
Are you into tapetrading by the way?
Anyway, that's all for now. I really hope to hear from you again...

Thrash

REPUGNANT
c/o Tobias Forge

PS.If you'll reply this letter, would you please return my glued stamps?

afield for the next generation of bands, although in a sadly ironic twist, it would be the same scenario as had happened with the likes of Sleep and At The Gates, in that while Earache were perfectly able to find the next big thing, years would be required before press and media alike caught up with Dig's vision.

"There was a weird period from about 1996 onwards where the death metal boom waned," Dig comments, "[and] many people assumed we'd shuttered the doors or gone bankrupt, which we came close to doing. Many of the key players of the label's early years took a hiatus or a decade-long time out from the scene, jumping ship back to a 'normal' life. Examples include Jeff Walker working a normal nine-to-five job in a bank after Carcass' split, Brutal Truth splitting and Danny Lilker becoming a cab driver in New York. Karl Willetts also entered the Birmingham drum and bass scene – though Bolt Thrower, to their credit, carried on.

"Sleep imploded completely," Dig continues, "with Matt Pike continuing as High on Fire, Justin Broadrick folded Godflesh, At The Gates split and re-grouped as The Haunted, David Vincent joined industrial shock-merchants Genitorturers, and Nicke Andersson [Entombed] found success with the rock 'n' roll of The Hellacopters. ▶

"I THINK IT REINVIGORATED BOTH NAPALM DEATH AND MORBID ANGEL, AND IT WAS A KICK UP THE ARSE FOR US."

Deicide

Oli Sykes

With most of Earache's acts split up or moved on, Pearson admits, "the label was decimated; it was a dark time. The years 1996-2007 were a triple-whammy body-blow of black metal rising, a new rap/nu-metal movement beginning to monopolise the metal scene and, to make matters worse still, the MP3 file downloading digital revolution hurting traditional sales. Earache more or less went into survival mode; focusing on re-packaging past albums, investing in DVDs and even a PlayStation 2 game Earache Extreme Metal Racing came out, we were diversifying as best we could.

"By 2005 or so, the landscape for an extreme metal band was much rosier, partly due to the file sharing revolution going on," he adds. "MySpace helped, but I think the real attraction was a lucrative live touring and festival circuit for extreme bands had developed, which did not exist a decade beforehand. Luckily, Earache came out the other side unscathed, catalogue intact. We re-emerged a leaner and meaner business to boot."

Casting their net nearer home, Digby noticed Sheffield-based metalcore combo Bring Me The Horizon making waves on the then fashionable MySpace. This is perhaps hard to fathom now given the band's current status, but having freshly signed to Visible Noise, BMTH met incredible resistance from the established metal scene at the time, with Visible Noise label manager Julie Weir finding it all but impossible to drum up interest Stateside.

Digby explains "The band was considered an unknown, online entity, possibly a flash in the pan, but every day I took the bus to my office, I saw kids get on wearing BMTH merch, fringed hair, the lot. I saw with my own eyes, this fanbase was real."

Earache reached out to license the debut album 'Count Your Blessings' for the USA via a Visible Noise license deal.

"YOU HAVE TO REMEMBER THAT THE BAND WAS IN DISARRAY AT THE TIME."

"I thought it was some kids trying to sound like The Dillinger Escape Plan, but I thought: 'let's do it'," Al Dawson says. "It was a fairly low-cost deal. They're one of the biggest rock bands in the world right now, but at the time, they weren't really seen as being legitimate artists to the older fans.

"He [Oli Sykes, singer] was charged with pissing on a girl in Nottingham, so I talked to him on the phone. What he said was that this girl was an annoying hanger-on and had got onto their bus. She wouldn't leave, and in the end opened the toilet door while he was pissing. He turned around in shock, and a little bit got on her.

"So it wasn't a Vince Neil escapade. We needed the band to tour and it cost at least $4000-$5000 [just] on work permits and lawyers. The only thing we could do was hope that the charges would be dismissed and, as it turned out, the drummer's visas got delayed causing him to miss the tour, but Oli made it out.

"Most bands you play a couple of small dates before you play New York, but BMTH's first date is in New

PlayStation 2
EARACHE
EXTREME METAL RACING
12+

Cult Of Luna

York opening for Kittie. The venue was BB King's, which was smack in the middle of 42nd Street. They didn't tell me until they arrived that they needed a drummer! So I found this session drummer who got their set down in six hours, so I was pretty worried.

"The venue was full of suburban moms dropping off their kids. The audience was 90 percent female and under 21. After their set, half the kids emptied out. I went home very impressed and wrote this long email to Dig saying this band were going to be massive. The album came out and we got their first week sales. 200 copies! The next week 100 copies. Dig flipped! We ended up doing 80,000 copies, and that was after the crash in the music industry. They did the Vans Warped Tour and were doing $50k a night in merchandise sales. Some bands just about manage that in one tour."

Sweden's Cult Of Luna were another band signed to Earache who, while influenced by the classic Earache albums, didn't necessarily fit with the Earache brand at first glance.

"Without Earache, I don't think we would be the band we are today," says guitarist Johannes Persson. "One of the most important things at that point was having a label that paid for tour support. In the long run, that meant a whole lot. We played with some strange bands over the years, but we were able to play a lot. We played with melodic hardcore bands, The Dillinger Escape Plan, The Haunted; we toured with everyone. That helped us to really understand that how to get anywhere was to go out there and play.

"These days, we've done everything but back then, everything seemed so cool," he continues. "I'm talking about touring in a night-liner and having a tour manager for the first time. They flew us over to the UK [especially] to play a show at Rock City in Nottingham with free booze. All those new experiences, that's what I associate with Earache. That was all super exciting [for us]! I met a whole bunch of amazing people through Earache and I still consider them good friends." ♠

CHAPTER NINE
XMAS PARTY PUNCH UP

WORDS BY
SAM BEAN

The Berzerker

The Berzerker

Earache held some legendary Xmas parties; here's Sam Bean of The Berzerker's account of 2002's:

"The Berzerker headlined the Earache Christmas Party in 2002. True to form, we acted like dicks. Here's what I remember.

"We were at the end of our first UK tour, and we looked and smelled like homeless bums who had stolen a bunch of music equipment. The tour was closing out with a headline appearance at the annual Earache Christmas Party in their hometown of Nottingham. The venue for the party was Rock City. We were actually really excited about the gig for about ten minutes or so until someone told us that we weren't actually playing on the main stage. We were to be playing in a small side-room instead.

"There was one glorious feature of that tour: it was sponsored by Jägermeister. Countless cases of Jägermeister had been crammed into the back of the tour bus along with promotional Jägermeister t-shirts, which we plundered in lieu of doing laundry. Every night started off with two ginormous bottles of Jägermeister that we were supposed share around with people. Naturally we shared it primarily amongst ourselves. This proved to be a wise investment on Jägermeister's part because I've been addicted to the filthy stuff ever since, and they have more than made their money back from me alone. In true touring style, venues would only give us a little water and no juice or soft drink so everyone ended up subsisting on the Jäger. We had Earache's previous PR girl Jo to thank for the hook-up, so I ensured that she was thanked. Then her replacement Sarah came up to have a word with us.

"Sarah is a small alternative chick with short hair who wears a beanie most of the time. She took us aside to share some DO's and DON'Ts with us. I only remember one of them, and that was because it seemed so completely ridiculous: basically, she told us not to terrorize Cult Of Luna. They're a Swedish alt-rock metal, slow-song bunch of boys who were on before us that night. Apparently they were afraid of us. Well not so much us, the masks. Sarah specifically forbade us from scaring them while we were wearing the masks. I thought she was joking. We'd just finished a US tour playing to thousands of people, none of whom seemed the least bit frightened. But she was dead-set finger-wagging serious. We nodded expressionlessly while I made a mental note to storm the stage wearing my mask during their set and try and bite as many of them as possible.

"We had to get masked up early in the afternoon as it turned out. Metal Hammer had sent a photographer to take shots of us both as the band and individually. The shots were done in the main room of Rock City and took around an hour all up. I forget exactly how it happened, but we decided to remain masked-up and creep around Rock City with the photographer following us, getting some action shots of us 'interacting with the environment'. The first thing we did was hunt down Sarah. We found her in the small side-room that the gig was going to be in. She was standing up on a bench near the wall putting up posters. We swarmed her and lifted her above our rubbery fanged heads and ran around going GRAAAAAH. She screamed uncontrollably. We were pleased.

"Our next target didn't go so well. Luke and I spotted Digby Pearson in the foyer of the venue, and the cameraman suggested that we grab Dig and do the same thing to him. Dig had cameras and handheld videos hanging around his neck and in his coat pockets. There were a few people around. The Metal Hammer photographer got in position. For those not in the know, Digby (aka Dig) is the head of Earache Records and was putting on the party at his own personal expense. Luke and I split up and started circling him, getting closer. I really don't know what our plan was now I think of it. Maybe wrestle him, take him down, and whoever had the best position could try and fit the top half of his head in the mouth of their mask and make it look like we were eating his brains. Dig saw us circling him and kind of smiled and went "what's going on here?" We lunged in. Luke went for the top half; I went for his legs. The photographer got in close and started snapping.

"Dig fucking lost it. The first thing I realized was that he was not going down. He was fighting like his life depended on it. I became aware that he was quite a bit heavier than me and bucking wildly. Luke backed off and I felt some seriously heavy punches whistle past my face. When you can wear a few inches

Earache staff at Xmas Party & Mark / Freebase

"YOU THINK THAT'S FUCKING FUNNY DO YOU? YOU TRY THAT ON ME AGAIN YOU LITTLE CUNT AND I'LL FUCKING KILL YOU"

of latex around your head but still feel the proximity of fisticuffs, you know they're not fucking around. I stepped back. Dig was red faced and furious and ready to kick some ass. Luke and the photographer went running off to the main room giggling like schoolboys and I raced after them.

"We convened there. Dig ran in after us, came straight up to me, and got right in my face and started yelling.

"You think that's fucking funny do you? You try that on me again you little cunt, and I'll FUCKING KILL YOU!"

"I was concerned. For all intents and purposes, this guy was our boss – buying our flights, paying bills, and responsible for our career. I'm not sure what response we were expecting from our half-hearted mugging attempt, but this wasn't it.

"Dig raced after the photographer next. "Give me that fucking film!"

"The photographer, who was a credit to his profession, replied, "Who the fuck are you?"

"The guy paying your fucking bills!" Dig snapped.

"At this point Luke stepped in and they all moved to the other side of the room for a chat. I watched the back and forth go for a while and couldn't really make out what was going on. Whatever Luke said seemed to calm everything down a bit, 'cause after a few minutes there was the metal handshake and Dig walked away a bit calmer than he'd arrived. Once he was downstairs Luke turned to me and started pissing himself laughing.

"HAHAHAHAHAHA! Ahhhhahahaha wasn't that the FUNNIEST thing you've ever seen? HAHAHAHAHA"

"I was like, I don't know. We'd made a sport of hassling Dig and ripping on him ever since we'd started with the label…but this felt like we'd pushed it too far. Or had we?

"What just happened?" I said.

"Ah, he said he was worried because he had lots of expensive camera equipment on him and stuff, and he thought it was going to get broken when we went after him. Or something like that." Luke said dismissively. "He wanted those photos deleted as well, once they were gone he calmed down a bit."

"The photographer came over and smirked. "Didn't get all of them, though". He showed us a few snaps of us brawling with our record label manager on the floor.

"The rest of the show got blurry. I started necking little minibar bottles of Jägermeister that were floating around, breaking my rule of no preshow drinks. At the insistence of Labrat's Martin Ives, I ▶

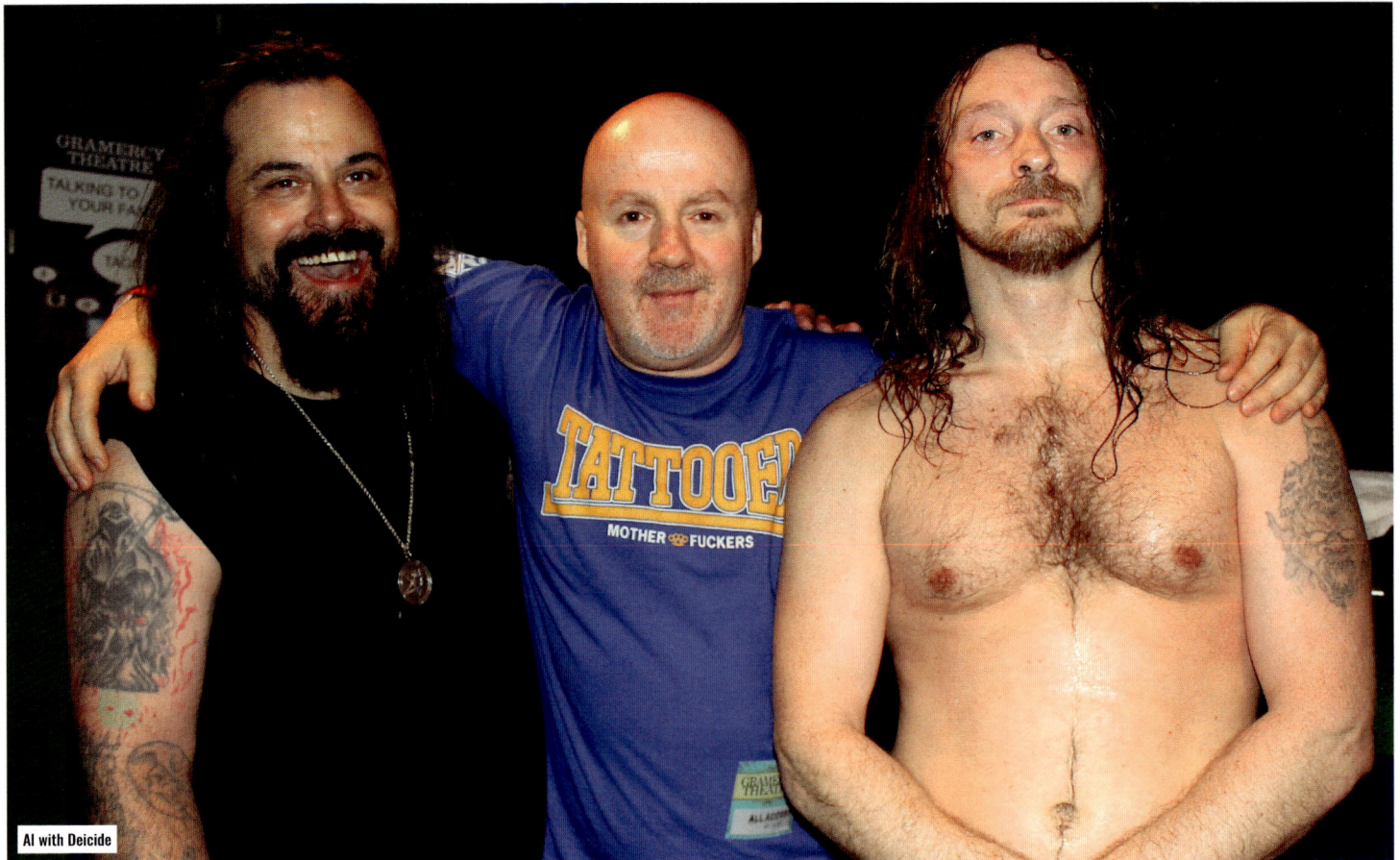

Al with Deicide

watched Cult Of Luna (maskless). He proclaimed their songs to be like "ten-minute long orgasms", leading me to deduce that he had the libido of a Galápagos turtle on sedatives. That was back in the day where I had zero tolerance for any slow metal.

"Luke absolutely loathed Cult Of Luna. The label had organized cameramen to film our show for the upcoming 'Principles and Practices of The Berzerker' DVD, and the venue had some stupid British curfew rule where they'd ring the bell, turn the lights on, and kick everyone out. Bands had to be punctual. We didn't want our live performance for the DVD to cut out halfway through with the lights getting turned on and some muppet ringing a bell. Cult Of Luna not only played overtime – understandable, seeing as though they play at 20bpm – but did one of those rockstar endings where they make a great big wall of noise and feedback, put their instruments down while still plugged in, and walked off. Yes, bravo guys. We waited for them to come back and pack up, but they didn't reappear. Luke stormed backstage to find them and tell them to get rid of their stuff so we could set up, but they'd vanished. Eventually he found them out the back of the venue and screamed at them to clear their shit off.

"Afterwards, I found Dig and made my peace with him. We posed for a photo with him getting me in a headlock. I figured we were square. I had a chat with Rob or Dan from Earache, and they mentioned Mick Kenney from Anaal Nathrakh was at the party. I went squeeeee and demanded we be introduced. I had heard 'The

Codex Necro" a few months previously and thought "at last…..we have some competition!" Retrospect is hilarious, isn't it?"

[Reprinted by permission of Sam Bean (The Berzerker bassist)]

Earache's next 'death metal' move was a surprise to many long-time observers. Having spent many years nurturing young bands and taking them up several levels, for the first time in the label's history, Dig signed a 'heritage' act to the label. Deicide had found fame in a blaze of publicity, issuing some strong albums, but over the years had seen their stock decline due to an increasingly acrimonious working relationship between bassist/vocalist Glen Benton and drummer Steve Asheim on one side and the Hoffman brothers – Brian and Eric, both guitarists – on the other ("My famous saying back then was that I'm not fucking Rumpelstiltskin and I can't spin your fucking shit into gold!" laughs Benton). A similarly deteriorating relationship with their then record label had also taken hold.

"It's no secret that when you're on your last record for a record company that's been sticking it up your ass for any number of years, you ain't gonna be breaking out your best shit," Benton smiles. "You just want to get the hell off of the label."

"So we dropped Morbid Angel and picked up Deicide!" Dan enthuses. "That was good fun. What was good about that was that Deicide were making terrible records at that point, and we got stuck into them. There was a trading of ideas and we really raised them up again. Glen was great fun. They toured Europe straight ▶

Glen Benton live

after we had signed them. I went to meet them in Bradford, and we had prepared a little gift for the guys; special T-shirts that were a play on the warning message they used to put on the back of all their Roadrunner LPs – 'Stop The Madness - Drugs Are No Fun'. We amended it to: 'Start The Madness - Christians Are No Fun'!

"Eventually, after standing around for 30 minutes Glen came bowling through the crowd looking like a completely unapproachable crazy guy, and I think: 'Right, best go speak to him'. I stop him, explain who I am, and hand him the shirts. He looks at me like I'm some kind of idiot, takes the shirts and looks at it all frowning and totally unfriendly. He sees the message and breaks into a massive smile, laughing out loud: 'That's cool, man!'

"Glen was a total character; mad as anything, but great," Tobin continues. "I remember we got him interviewed for a BBC documentary called Death Metal Murders as Deicide were supposed to have been a big influence on the killers. For years no one had asked Glen about his branding [of an inverted crucifix into his forehead], and this bloke asked: 'Did it hurt?' Glen just deadpanned: 'Yes'."

Released in 2004, the 'Scars Of The Crucifix' album hit UK sales of well over ten times those achieved for its Roadrunner Record predecessor 'In Torment In Hell', Deicide, on paper at least, looked to be back and firing on all cylinders. The touring undertaken at the time displayed a band seemingly far more relaxed and more professional, perfectly at ease with the job in hand and more than ready to take on all-comers. Underneath,

> **"SO WE DROPPED MORBID ANGEL AND PICKED UP DEICIDE."**

though, there was turmoil with Glen becoming increasingly exasperated by his deteriorating relationship with the Hoffman brothers, to the point where he was seriously questioning the point of the band.

"We thought it was [more confident]", Benton says of the era, "but there was a storm on the horizon. Where it was going was inevitable; for me I was almost ready to hang my hat. I'd been managing the band and doing all that shit myself for years, with no appreciation from anybody apart from Steve. It had got to a point where I was questioning who I was doing this for."

Outside of Deicide, Benton had been a part of the 'Dechristianize' album, released by the band Vital Remains, and, he admits, "I was really looking for a way out, so when the Hoffmans quit they did me a huge favour."

The three albums recorded by the band for Earache showed that Deicide were still more than capable of writing some outstanding material and, despite a tumultuous time via a series

The Berzerker

of line-up changes, personal problems and touring issues, both group and label look on their time together with fondness and pride, something that even Glen's non-appearance on their final European tour while signed to Earache has failed to diminish.

"Unfortunately ''Till Death Do Us Part' was our last record with Earache and I was just going through my second divorce and a major custody battle," Glen recalls. "I can't say that Earache were especially happy to hear about that, but I had to go to custody for my kid because his mother wasn't up to doing the job and I had to step up and take the bull by the horns. For me, that was just a studio record. Steve wrote all of the music and I wrote all of the lyrics. I wrote them about what I was going through at the time. I have to have misery in my life to write lyrics. That and a lot of weed!"

Glen's electing to stay home was something for which no-one had received prior warning, least of all a certain Earache press officer who had, thanks to the band's improved standing within the extreme metal world, managed to secure Deicide (and Glen in particular) a healthy amount of press coverage.

"They had some Eastern European stand-in who wasn't up to scratch," remembers Dan Tobin, "[and] the problem was that because the band was going so well, we had lots of media interest and we had secured a review of the Manchester show in The Guardian. I was supposed to meet the writer, chuff him up and make sure the show got a good review. I promised him he could meet Glen, and witness the madness for himself, I really hammered it up; 'Glen's crazy, he's a livewire'.

"At the venue I found the writer all excited about meeting Glen," he continues. "I say: 'Give me five minutes and go into the dressing room to find there's no Glen. When I asked the guys where he was and they casually replied: 'Glen didn't come, he's at home'. I had to think double-fast because not only was the writer waiting outside expecting to meet Satan himself, the band were getting ready to go on with some no-name stand in singer."

Perhaps inevitably, things got worse.

"After the initial portion of this, he ran out of songs to sing!" Tobin relates, still sounding bamboozled. "Jack [Owen, guitarist] may have sung one or two, they played an instrumental song, and then the band started getting kids up from the crowd to do 'karaoke Deicide' - all of this in front of The Guardian!"

"We had a lot of good times," says Glen. "Dig took us out [to a bar] one time when we were over there. We had an awesome time. It ended up with me jumping off the bar, chewing glass, doing my usual antics, and then I went back and trashed the hotel room. Great times, man! They wanted to get me all liquored up – 'Let's see what he's like when you pour Jack Daniel's in him'. Now they know! There was a crowd, then people started dissipating; the drunker we got, the more people started heading for the door!"

Dan Tobin remembers that night well: "We started drinking and as the night went on their behaviour got worse and worse. Somehow people found out Glen was at the pub, and the phone started ringing, people phoning up to shout abuse down the phone at him, and he would be challenging them to come down and

Glen Benton

fight, bring all their friends down and fight as well! Then he got on the bar and basically stage-dived into the table we were sitting at, beer and glass everywhere. I think Dig said to him: 'Come on Glen, eat that pint glass' and he did! It was Glen's way of saying: 'Don't fuck with me, I'm crazy!'

"To be honest, although I was shocked, we took it in our stride," laughs Dan. "We had dealt with plenty of crazies before and Glen was just another in a long line of them. In our world, doing the music we do, it's [been] par for the course. The madder strands of society tend to gravitate towards us! Glen was and still is a larger than life personality. He clearly lives life by his own rules and won't take shit from anyone, but you have to give him credit as a lifer. The guy never caved in, he never quit. He kept his band alive."

"When it comes to bad blood with labels, I have no bad blood with them," concludes Glen. "They take care of me. I did something that Dig got offended by but I was just joking; I took some photos of my dog taking a poop and had the Earache logo coming out his asshole while he was pooping and mass emailed it to everyone," he laughs. "I do apologise to him for that, it was just my sick sense of humour!" ♠

Benji Webbe

REDEFINNG EXTREMITY ONCE AGAIN

With their death metal empire crumbling, Earache Records was about to set a new course. What would follow over the course of a decade or two was a slow but steady reinvention of all that the label had stood for.

Dub War continued the label's interest in bands that functioned outside of the box. Fronted by the irrepressible Benji Webbe, they were influenced jointly by rock, punk, rap and reggae, standing out like sore thumbs in the post-grunge fallout.

"Dub War just wanted to do something a bit different to what else was going on," Webbe explains of a spiky but unapologetic style that pooled the best bits of The Clash, Bob Marley and the seminal underground black US hardcore crew Bad Brains, topped off by thought-provoking lyrical messages.

"There was a lot of interest around us from companies that were bigger than Earache," Webbe recalls, "but out of the blue Digby turned up in Newport at one of our rehearsal sessions. Frankly, none of us knew anything at all about Earache Records because it was outside of our circle – at that time they were still releasing the really heavy stuff – but he said all of the right things.

"Digby told us that he'd already seen a few of our shows without approaching us, which we were really impressed by," Webbe continues. "Within a couple of weeks we were in the studio recording the first Dub War album."

Many eyebrows have been raised over new additions to the label's roster since Earache's post-millennial reinvention, but at the time the signing of Dub War was viewed as every bit as unlikely.

"There are many parallels between what we did with Dub War and what later happened with Rival Sons," Dan Tobin believes. "Dub War was a huge move away from the old guard of Carcass, Napalm, Bolt Thrower and all that stuff, because that era was coming to a close. Just in the same way that Rival Sons signalled a change at a time when the thrash bands and trad metal bands like Municipal Waste, Evile and White Wizzard had almost exhausted their potential."

Dub War themselves were aware of the perceived novelty factor. Benji laughs: "Back then I was a born again Christian. Some friends of mine said: 'Fucking hell, Dig's going to sign Cliff Richard next'!"

A full-length debut, 'Pain', was issued in 1995, followed a year later by 'Wrong Side Of Beautiful', a follow-up that brought out a slightly mellower and more commercial side of the band's make-up. The singles began to sell; 'Enemy Maker' peaking agonisingly outside of the national Top 40 at #41 though Dub War also attained success with 'Strike It', 'Cry Dignity' and 'Million Dollar Love'.

"As an alternative reggae punk-rock band we were a bit strange for those that usually bought Earache products, but things began to build," Benji recalls.

"Everyone at Earache had thought 'Enemy Maker' a strong song; it had that very basic The Police-style groove to it," says Tobin. "This was my first experience of Dig throwing everything we had at it, he told me once that he had 'bet the company' on Dub War – meaning the amount of work he put in and the amount of investment put in was very high. A lot of money was spent."

Dan Tobin recalls watching from the wings as Dub War played for an estimated 135,000 people on the main stage at the Dynamo Festival in Holland in 1995. "It had been raining and a wall of steam came off the crowd, they were churning up the mud and going absolutely crazy," he says. "It really felt as though the band was going to become big. Benji had got a lot of recognition from fellow musicians like Max Cavalera and Robert Trujillo – he later guested on a project of Robert's called Mass Mental – and it seemed like the minds of the fans were opening up."

In the summer of 1997, the group's newfound status resulted in the offer of a set at Glastonbury Festival, and the band also played support on a tour for the Manic Street Preachers' album 'The Holy Bible'.

"Glastonbury was the biggest show that we'd ever played but on the day there was a drummer malfunction; too many drugs or whatever. But the end result was that he couldn't play so a friend of ours, Jon Lee from Feeder – God rest his soul – was prepared to get up and have a go at busking it," Benji winces, adding: "The conditions under which we did that Manics tour were a nightmare, but looking back now, we didn't realise that we were onto something real good."

Earache had hired radio pluggers to promote the band's singles, but the era's press couldn't get their heads around what was going on.

"It was incredibly frustrating to work this very talented and credible group, with a fantastic frontman in Benji and yet to meet such resistance from the mainstream media," says Tobin, who ran the band's printed media campaign. "The NME was featuring bands like Skunk Anansie, Placebo, Reef and all of the Britpop bands of course, but they would not take Dub War seriously."

Earache assembled their brightest stars of the era for a European tour billed as Earache: Next Gen98. Dub War were headliners, and also on the bill were Misery Loves Co., Janus Stark, Pulkas

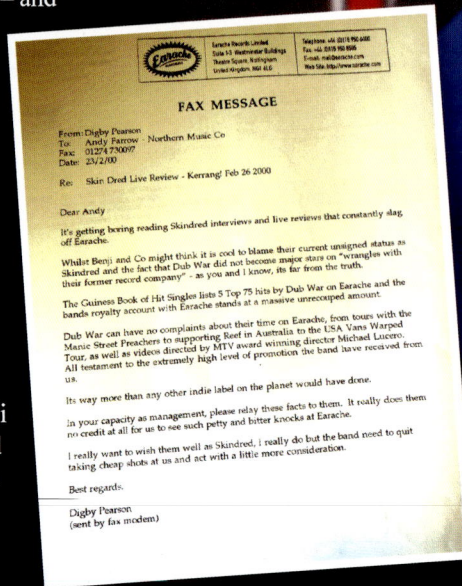

Dub War

and Ultraviolence. This was about as un-traditional a line-up as one could imagine.

"Misery Loves Co were riding high in an era when bands like Fear Factory and Machine Head were showing a new way forward for metal," Tobin says. "Pulkas were also very much on the cutting edge being compared to Tool and alt-rock – and they were selling records. Janus Stark were on the poppier side but Gizz was in The Prodigy and had a lot of attention. Ultraviolence was just out there, really – a fascination of Dig's from the hardcore gabba techno scene."

The trek's UK shows were well received, though as Tobin notes: "We struggled in places like Germany, but Next Gen98 was an example of Earache's willingness to try new things and to be a little different."

"AS AN ALTERNATIVE REGGAE PUNK-ROCK BAND WE WERE A BIT STRANGE FOR THOSE THAT USUALLY BOUGHT EARACHE PRODUCTS."

Napalm Death

Summer (Earache USA staffer) and Jose (Bonded By Blood)

Anders Björler – The Riff Machine

Dan Hardy / UFC Fighter

Earache time capsule

"THE ERA'S PRESS COULDN'T GET THEIR HEADS AROUND WHAT WAS GOING ON."

There was an attempt to break the band in the States when Dub War played three weeks on the bill of Warped, a festival bill that travelled across the country, followed by three weeks of shows with Fishbone and Snot.

"Ultimately, once the 'Enemy Maker' single failed to chart, I think Dig felt that after several singles and videos and expensive campaigns, he was never gonna see the band break through," Tobin recalls. "That was a real shame because they were certainly among the top live bands we ever had on the label."

When Dub War split in 1999 after one too many disputes with the company, Benji Webbe shared their air of frustration and disappointment.

"I was very angry that I had lost the band," he states now. "I blamed Digby and I blamed Earache and I said so in the press, but age is a great leveller and I know that without Earache it's more than likely I wouldn't have done anything in music."

Given the sour ending to what had threatened to be a rosy career, it's tempting to speculate upon how Dub War might have fared had they accepted one of the many offers from their bigger and more lucrative suitors.

"It's a great question," Benji laughs. "Sure, it's possible that we might have better chart positions but take a look back at those bands from 1995 and how many of them are still around?

"Being on Earache Records, I look back at that now and go: 'Wow'," he adds. "Digby gave us everything he had. The path I took with Dub War gave me longevity; it brought me a career. With hindsight it gave me credibility and that's something I really didn't think we had at the time."

In the aftermath of Dub War's dissolution Webbe, guitarist Jeff Rose and drummer Martin 'Ginge' Ford went on to form Skindred, though Rose and Ford didn't stay the course. However, Skindred have become a force to be reckoned with, rebooting the Dub War blueprint for a new generation of fans and establishing themselves among the biggest acts on the summer festival scene. With six albums to their name, some of which were issued via major labels, any hostilities of the past are pretty much forgotten.

"Earache gave Dub War so much," Benji now enthuses, "and it's funny – many of the friends that I made back in those days are still among those closest to me. Honestly, at all of the numerous labels I've been with since [as a member of Skindred] I've never had those kinds of relationships with label managers or A&R people at all."

"Ultimately, Benji re-invented himself with Skindred and much as I love them too, I can't help hearing Dub War in their sound now," Tobin confesses. "And it's hard not to wonder why they made it and Dub War failed to do so." ◆

Linea 77

CHAPTER ELEVEN
NU-METAL DABBLING

Klas Rydberg / Cult Of Luna

Earache had an enviable knack of discovering and signing a succession of different acts. Much of this was attributable to Hugh Jones, who joined the label in June 1996 to help with the sale of merchandise. Later promoted by Digby to a role as an A&R man, Jones was also a deejay at Nottingham Rock City and his almost unquenchable thirst for new talent led to a highly productive five-year spell. Indeed, Andy Copping calls Jones "a massively influential guy with his finger right on the pulse of the music."

Jones was among the first in the know when it came to the likes of Papa Roach, Korn, Linkin Park and Limp Bizkit. "Okay, Earache weren't able to sign any of those bands because the majors had bigger chequebooks, but to me it showed the vision that they had," Copping says. "Hugh was right there in the midst of all."

"As a teenager back in the 1980s I had trawled through Metal Forces magazine looking for demos and at Earache I was forever telling them about new bands I'd heard," Jones says. "When Korn came out with 'Blind' and Deftones put out 'Seven Words' that was really interesting music. We would have a couple of thousand kids going nuts at Rock City and it began a broadening of the genre's horizons which I considered a great thing, but of course like every scene it became stale after a while.

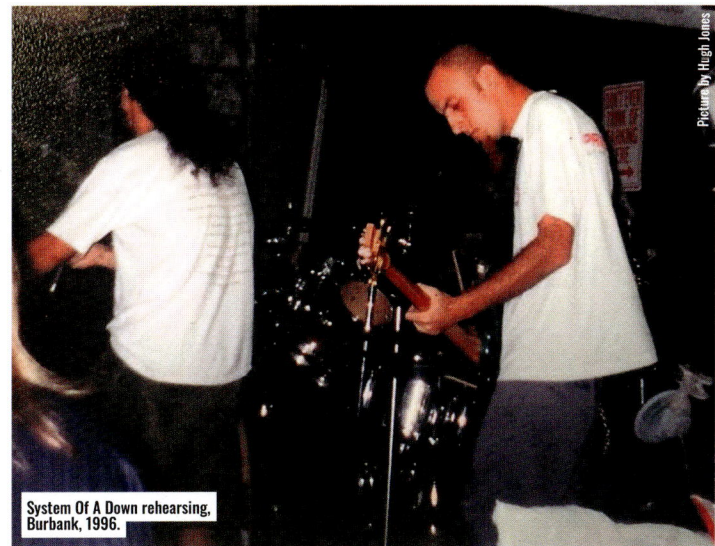
System Of A Down rehearsing, Burbank, 1996.

Picture by Hugh Jones

Linkin Park friended you on Myspace
14 June 2012 20:15

myspace.

Hey Earache Records,

Linkin Park friended you on Myspace.

Accept Ignore

View Linkin Park's profile

Mitch Dickinson

"My contacts were pretty good," he adds. "Dino Cazares from Fear Factory was a good friend and he passed me a lot of recommendations, although quite a few of them I didn't really like – we're talking about bands like Spineshank."

Jones still has no fondness for the term 'nu-metal' – "I prefer heavy-alternative," he says – but he was among the first talent scouts to pay attention to System Of A Down, the Armenian-American band that would go on to sell millions of records. Indeed, in the summer of '96 he and Pearson flew out to Los Angeles for the industry free-for-all Foundations Forum, and also to investigate what was happening in the clubs.

"We looked at Snot before they signed to a major [the band's debut, 'Get Some', was issued by Geffen in 1997] and we also went to see Earth Crisis in Hollywood," he relates. "We were very interested in them, but Ozzy and Sharon Osbourne were there and we knew that they were going to form their own label, so it seemed there was little chance of making it happen."

It was at the Troubadour in West Hollywood that the pair experienced an early show from SOAD. "Two hundred Armenian kids were running around with flags, going absolutely crazy and Dig's mouth was wide open: 'We've got to get this band'," Jones recalls. "It was like Napalm Death at the Dome back in the late ▶

Woods Of Ypres

Dig with Benji

Evile at Bloodstock

Municipal Waste

1980s – just out of control. This was the future right in front of our eyes."

The Earache deposition went to the band's rehearsal room and they did what Hugh calls "the whole 'dinner at the Rainbow' thing", but as he explains: "After a while it because obvious that they were using us as fishing bait. They were associated with us in order to reel in all of the other labels. At their shows there were bigger labels turning up and after a while they stopped returning our calls. Eventually, we read that they were in New York with Rick Rubin and the rest of the story [their self-titled debut was issued by Rubin's American Records in 1998 – it's since sold more than a million copies] is well known."

Earache did sign at least one band from the scene – an Italian six-piece called Linea 77.

"A tape of their debut album ['Too Much Happiness Makes Kids Paranoid', 1998] which was released only in Italy appeared on my desk. It was great and available to license for a reasonable price," Jones explains. "At home they were playing to two thousand kids per night. So we booked them a little UK tour, it might have been with One Minute Silence, and they blew me away. We also released 'Ket.ch.up Sui.ci.de' [2000] and they got some reviews and charted high in the Italian Top 40, but unfortunately a lot of the UK kids at the time just wanted the American bands."

Gradually, interest in the so-called nu-metal scene began to fade as the kids looked for the next new fad. "From 1997 onwards,

with the likes of Linkin Park, it became really, really watered down," Jones says with distaste. "There was no heart and soul; it was dreadful."

"The reason we had dabbled with Dub War and Janus Stark was because Dig had looked at what was going on in the mainstream and wanted some of that: 'If all of those other bands are getting chart success then why can't we?' So he went for it and now it seems to have come full circle, look how well the label is doing now."

The story of Janus Stark and their unashamed pop-punk represents another vital chapter in the evolution of Earache Records. Not only was the trio's music vital, fresh and contemporary of its era, this was no pre-existing band that approached the label cap in hand, looking for a deal. Janus Stark were nurtured pretty much every step of the way from their formation to the release of an outstanding debut, 'Great Adventure Cigar', in May 1998.

Guitarist/frontman Gizz Butt had cut his teeth with Peterborough punks The Destructors before joining the English Dogs. In '96 he was hired as a live guitarist with The Prodigy, the chart-conquering dance-rock act that had become one of the world's biggest attractions thanks to that year's number one single 'Firestarter'.

"Being in The Prodigy at that particular moment in time caused me to think about music in a different way," considers Butt now. "Being with them as we travelled exposed me to lots of different ▶

sounds and styles and it really opened up my horizons."

"Gizz sent some of his songs through to Earache, and at the time he was really influenced by Dave Grohl and Foo Fighters," explains Hugh Jones. "They were really good and exciting."

After several months of discussion with Jones and Digby Pearson, finally, in the Peterborough living room of Gizz Butt, the label came to an agreement to greenlight the project. Butt had experienced being signed to Clay Records and the Music For Nations subsidiary Under One Flag during this time with the English Dogs, and save for some in-house criticism of his vocals further down the line Gizz has only positive words about his time with the company.

"Earache stood behind their investment," Butt believes. "They gave us a great advance and a good recording budget, and as the record label they did their bit. That's one of the reasons we felt so comfortable with them, there was a team around us."

Besides overseeing the album's production, Terry Thomas (not to be confused with the gap-toothed comedian of the same name) was appointed as Janus Stark's manager. Thomas brought an innate knowledge of songcraft. He had come from a melodic rock background, producing and writing for the likes of Bad Company and Foreigner before helping Brit rockers 3 Colours Red to score a run of Top 30 singles.

"We demoed a whole album's worth of material and it was fantastic; great choruses and well-written songs," Jones remembers. "At the end of the day there are only two types of music, good and bad, and Janus Stark were very good indeed."

If Janus Stark were making a play for the Foo Fighters market they couldn't have got a bigger boost than when Dave Grohl described them as "a great melodic kick up the ass."

"Yeah, Dave declared himself a fan, and at the time he was also a friend of mine," Butt states, "though looking back now, I saw us as being pitched somewhere between Therapy? and Helmet."

These were good times for the band and their label. To celebrate, Janus Stark headed out on the already mentioned Earache: Next Gen98 tour.

"We shared a bus with Dub War; Benji stayed downstairs because he didn't like the perpetual noise on the top deck," Butt smiles. "It was quite a rock 'n' roll tour. There was a huge table with everything on it and one day, for reasons that now escape me, I decided to run from the front of the bus and dive over it, impaling myself on several bottles. Dan Tobin came up the stairs telling us to turn down the racket and to my great shame I threw a bottle of Jack Daniel's right at him – it smashed inches from his

Beecher

The More I See on the original set of Star Wars

Ephel Duath

Municipal Waste

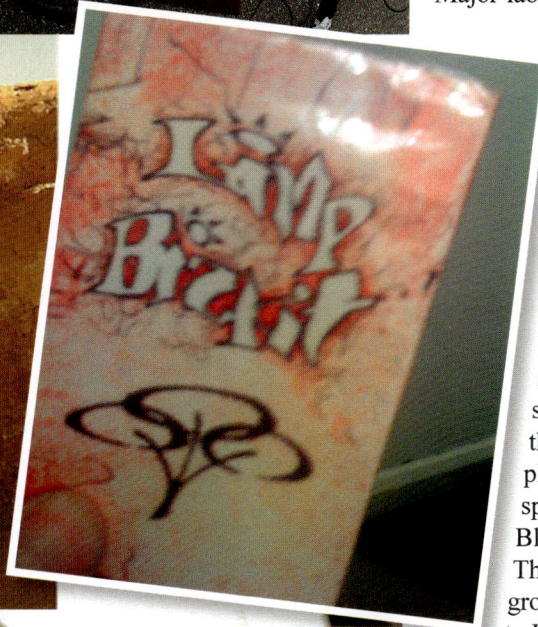

head. I don't think he will ever forgive me for that. We can laugh about now, but then he gives me that sideways glance of his."

Such was the album's crossover potential that Earache licensed 'Great Adventure Cigar' to the US label Trauma Records, home of Bush and No Doubt, and the band played a string of dates across the pond. Meanwhile, 'Every Little Thing Counts' appeared in the soundtracks to the movies Disturbing Behaviour and the Oscar nominated Varsity Blues. The latter was extremely welcome, admits Butt, as it gave him "the biggest royalty cheques of my entire musical career."

Things looked extremely positive for Janus Stark, but in the end the band fell apart purely through a mix of lack of available time and a lack of confidence to push onto the next level.

"In the early noughties we had to create a brand-new roster more or less from scratch as all the old guard had moved on. Major-label-led Nu-metal dominated the scene with Gothic metal being huge in Europe and Metalcore likewise in USA. Labels like Nuclear Blast and Relapse were kicking our arse with Nightwish and Mastodon. 2000s Metalcore just sounded like At The Gates copies to me, we didn't play that game, preferring to work with artists like Beecher and Ephel Duath as I thought they had more originality to them. Despite multiple albums their mathy/jazzy-core never caught on." Dig explains.

In its original guise, Thrash metal was a very American thing and in an unusual move, Earache signed Municipal Waste who were spearheading a return to the Thrash/Hardcore roots sound. Earache then signed a band that played the same type of music but with a British twist. Of all places, Evile came from Huddersfield. Dig had spotted them playing in an unsigned tent at the Bloodstock Festival and admired their raw potential. The band had begun life as Metal Militia, a tribute group that specialised in Metallica songs – thanks to Earache they would record a debut album, 2007's 'Enter The Grave', with that band's producer, Flemming Rasmussen.

"My first encounter with Earache was hearing Carcass," says guitarist/frontman Ol Drake. "I can't remember which pub I was in but I didn't know who it was so I asked. After that I got quite into death metal and came across Morbid Angel's early stuff. I think my first Earache purchase was 'Symphonies Of Sickness' by Carcass."

"When Earache signed Evile, thrash metal was basically a dead duck," Dan Tobin admits. However, Evile quickly forged a connection with both fans and the press, Kerrang! claiming that they were "carrying the genre's whole 'revival' on their shoulders."

Asked what Dig might have seen in Evile that set the band apart from the rest, Drake remains uncertain. "Possibly that we were doing everything ourselves and gigging a lot, and we weren't arseholes," he laughs. "Our songs were pretty fun live, too."

Evile

Janus Stark

Oceano's Adam Warren

Over the course of four albums Evile got to play with a string of prestigious headline acts including Megadeth, Machine Head, Sabbat and Job For A Cowboy. "A lot of that was due to being on Earache, being an Earache artist definitely made people take us a lot more seriously. They definitely opened many doors for us which we would never have been able to open by ourselves."

The death of Mike Alexander in 2009 was a hammer blow for all concerned. Evile had been on tour with Amon Amarth when the bassist was taken ill in Sweden. Tobin still recalls the disbelief at the call to inform him of the terrible news.

"Everybody in the office sat in silence for a long time," he sighs. "Even talking about it now brings back the chills that we felt. It was just so unfair – Mike was a lovely guy and completely dedicated to the band."

Being lumped in with so many other like-minded bands – many of them inferior – also began to take its toll as success eluded them.

"We were just playing the music we loved, we weren't reviving anything," Drake comments. "We grew slightly tired of being called retro-thrash, and started to try different things."

Besides Evile, Earache went all-in on numerous Thrash metal bands – SSS from Liverpool, Bonded By Blood from LA and of course Richmond, Virginia's own Municipal Waste, experiencing varying degrees of success with each. However, Municipal Waste became tired of being regarded as some sort of pizza-thrash novelty and expressed a desire to plough a more serious path. When their contract expired, despite Earache's offer being "far more than they were really worth" the band signed up elsewhere.

"In a weird way, that actually led us to re-think what we were doing," Tobin theorizes, "and what came next was Dig's complete 180-degree change of direction with the likes of Rival Sons and those more commercial bands." ♠

Picture by Pasi Rytkönen.

LABEL REBORN WITH THE BLUES

Rival Sons

From the perspectives of both label and artist, the importance of Rival Sons' signing to Earache is pretty much incalculable. The four-piece from Long Beach, California, were something completely different to anything that had gone before. As the first decade of the new millennium bled into the next, their blues-laden, groove-ridden hard rock sounded timeless. And yet despite being signed to a powerful management company the band was struggling to find any real traction.

A self-released album from 2009, 'Before The Fire', had picked up some positive reviews and Rival Sons were already established in what would become a long-term liaison with their producer Dave Cobb, but the all-important breakthrough seemed as far away as ever.

"We were still getting our sea legs together, and we had talked to a couple of different labels but nothing serious," explains guitarist Scott Holiday. "I had been signed to a couple of major labels before with other groups and the business was already starting to change – not as much as it has gone to change in the fullness of time, but we could see where it was starting to head. Signing to one of the majors really didn't appeal to me, so we ▶

Scott Holiday / Rival Sons

were figuring out the possibility of getting some investors and maybe doing things ourselves."

Dan Tobin still recalls the day that Pearson excitedly walked into the office brandishing a CD by a brand new band, Rival Sons, having found them on YouTube where they had a grand total of three clips online at the time. "He put it on for an opinion and it was great, but once it finished I asked him: 'What the hell has it got to do with us?' This wasn't an Earache band."

Despite indifference from his label manager, Pearson recognised that Earache had to get involved in the band, and instructed USA Label Manager Al Dawson to undertake intense negotiations to secure their signature with an exceptionally artist-friendly deal. "Here were the, to my ears at least, the best new rock band in the world, hands down. We had to work with them," says Pearson.

"The label had gone through a new wave of thrash with bands like Municipal Waste, Bonded By Blood and Gama Bomb, and then we signed Cauldron and Woods Of Ypres both from Canada. Woods attracted a fanbase after the singer David Gold tragically passed away'" says Al Dawson. "For Dig, that was almost like a whole new concept – wow, people that can really sing. From then on we only signed acts with exceptional vocalists"

"In a way [pursuing Rival Sons] made complete sense," he adds, "because heavy metal came from the blues. It was only later on when we signed The White Buffalo that I was fazed. If you told me ten years ago that we'd have a singer-songwriter on the label… well, that was impossible."

"THE IMPORTANCE OF RIVAL SONS' SIGNING TO EARACHE IS PRETTY MUCH INCALCULABLE."

Blackberry Smoke

Rival Sons

When Dawson got in touch with Rival Sons the band had very little background information about Earache, and, recalls Tobin, their approach "was very quickly dismissed. But we kept an eye on the situation because we couldn't understand why a band managed by Irving Azoff wasn't going anywhere."

"I knew of some of the earlier heavy bands that Earache had signed, but I had very little recognition of the label itself," Holiday says, echoing the words of several acts that would follow his band down a similar path over the coming years. "When I heard they were coming in for a band like ourselves I went away and did a little research and my first response was that they were kidding. The second was that it was hilarious. I mean, we are a soulful, blues-based rock 'n' roll band and this hardcore death metal label wanted to sign us – that appealed to my sense of humour. I told my manager: 'This is a joke, right?' Only they were deadly serious."

The first face-to-face interaction between band and label came when Earache's Dawson checked out an unusual gig at a place in New York's Lower East Side called Pianos.

"It was just a small place, almost a wine bar – quite sophisticated," Al laughs at the memory. "We wore nice, smart shirts with buttons instead of Morbid Angel or Deicide T-shirts. There were probably 40 or 50 people in the crowd but most of them were like: 'Ooh look at me, I'm a model' or they were TV directors or something."

Dawson knew that what he saw and heard that night was "a diamond in the rough", and after Earache were first rebuffed the label's intention became much clearer when they returned with what Scott Holiday now terms "a real offer".

"At that point we said: 'Okay, well… alright'," he laughs. "It seemed weird enough that it might just work, and we started listening. I saw how well they had done within the genre that they were known for and we decided to give it a shot. I liked the idea of our band being a black sheep on that label, it seemed interesting and audacious."

▶

"Tom Consolo, the band's day-to-day manager, told me that he couldn't get Rival Sons arrested at any of the major labels," confides Dawson. "What Tom liked about Earache was that it's an owner-operated indie label, and the owner of the company was a fan of the band. Eventually they agreed to a one-album deal which was later renewed several times."

"The only proviso they demanded was having complete one hundred per cent artistic freedom" Tobin adds, "and that wasn't going to be a problem."

One of the first things that Earache did was put on a gig at London's Barfly in February 2011, with support from Vintage Trouble. A buzz had already begun to build. Tobin had been to see the decision-makers at Classic Rock magazine, previewing a half-dozen of the best songs that the group had recorded.

"Right after that meeting Classic Rock were on the phone saying how amazing they thought the band was," he recalls, "though the people at Planet Rock took a little longer to convince. The first response we got back from them was: 'They sound like Kingdom Come'."

Tobin had to go away and perform a Google search on Kingdom Come, the German-American band whose 1980s impersonation of Led Zeppelin can only be described as 'audacious'. "Nobody can deny that Rival Sons were influenced by Zeppelin," he laughs, "but that comment horrified me."

Earache released the second Rival Sons album, 'Pressure And Time', in June 2011. Its cover art was provided by Storm Thorgerson (Led Zeppelin, Pink Floyd, Wishbone Ash and many more), though Dan Tobin still goes into a cold sweat when discussing how this arrangement came to pass. Before dying in 2013, Thorgerson had long since ceased working for just anybody. He was also known in the business as a very difficult man to deal with.

"I met Storm in a pub in Loughborough," Dan relates. "He had recently had a stroke and was wheeled in a chair by his partner in crime Aubrey Powell, also a pretty legendary guy. At one point I asked whether he had ever designed any covers he didn't like – I brought up Helloween's 'Pink Bubbles Go Ape' as being particularly shit, which he took umbrage to.

"When I explained that we had no budget but that the band were big fans of his work, he agreed to take the music away and listen to it. Back at the office I fired off an email to the Rival Sons manager explaining that I thought Storm might come on board for the project. I was in a rush and I'd had a couple of drinks

in the pub with Storm. My email said that I thought we could get Storm and get him on a budget that would suit us. I might have used the phrase: 'I'm going to lowball Storm Thorgerson' referring to the cost. And then I hit 'send'."

Almost instantaneously Tobin was struck by a horrible, paralysing fear that he had copied Thorgerson on the message.

"Had I really sent one of the most iconic album cover masterminds of the 20th Century an email saying that I was gonna 'lowball' him?" Dan says now, still chilled by the possibility. "On top of that I would also have embarrassed Rival Sons' manager, too. It took me ten minutes to check whether I had indeed copied Storm – and I hadn't, thank fuck."

The following morning Thorgerson said he would design the sleeve. "That was an important moment because it showed the band that Earache could deliver big names to work on their projects," Tobin comments. "It's such a shame that the resulting cover was among the worst ever released by Earache in my opinion."

> ## "I LIKED THE IDEA OF OUR BAND BEING A BLACK SHEEP ON THAT LABEL, IT SEEMED INTERESTING AND AUDACIOUS."

Earache's press team adapted quickly once again, now dealing with what was to all intents and purposes a brand new Rock n Roll scene, which was the home of legacy acts and traditionally bore little interest in new bands. Digby explains the dilemma, "to Rock radio and print gatekeepers, Rolling Stone and the like, you're not considered Classic Rock until you'd been around 20 plus years, yet here we were promoting a two-year old act, convinced they were the saviours of Classic Rock n Roll, quite audacious in hindsight."

Luckily, Rival Sons' musical authenticity and songwriting prowess spoke for itself and rock n roll media embraced them quickly.

"After Rival Sons had signed the contract and before I met the band, I hooked up with Tom Consolo in the UK with another of his acts, Meat Loaf," Tobin relates. "Meeting him at a show at Birmingham NEC was a world away from the likes of Municipal Waste or Enforcer gigs. There was huge catering, the crew backstage were watching golf, there was red wine instead of cheap lager, and a professional air that I must say appealed to me. I felt like dealing with these people could be a step up in a professional sense, and I knew we could cope with it."

Musically as well as ethically speaking, Rival Sons differed greatly from the rest of their label-mates.

"One of the things that we talked about a lot with Rival Sons at the beginning was 'what they stood for' – they're not a political band like say ►

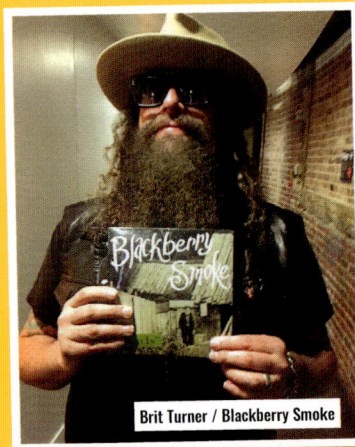

Brit Turner / Blackberry Smoke

Blackberry Smoke

Tim Commerford (Wakrat / RATM) and Tom Hadfield (Earache)

Brit Turner / Blackberry Smoke

Napalm Death, and we needed some angles in order to make them appear interesting to the media," Tobin explains. "One thing they were big on was being vegetarian and in some cases vegan, so we played on that for a while.

"At some point I got a call from our German partners who said that they could do something cool with the 'Pressure And Time' video. Their idea was to place the video in a nationwide chainstore, which would put the clip on their instore TV channel, on multiple rotation. There were approximately a thousand such stores across Germany, with a potential audience of millions. It seemed like good promotion – except the chainstore in Germany was called Burger King.

"Obviously that was at odds with the band's ethos, but I reasoned that being vegans they were unlikely to ever venture into a Burger King. The pay-off of millions people seeing the video seemed worth the risk."

Fast forward to the band's first ever UK festival appearance at Sonisphere 2011, where Rival Sons were playing the tiny Jägermeister stage for just a couple of hundred of people.

"Right before their set Scott Holiday came up to me and demanded: 'I need to talk to you once we're done'," Tobin relates. "My heart sank 'cos it sounded like he wanted to moan about something, so I was racking my brains thinking: 'What have I done now?'

"After the set here comes Scott: 'I need to talk to you about Germany…'

"'Uh-oh', I'm thinking – it's got to be Burger King. And sure enough he starts up: 'I was in Burger King in Cologne the other day and guess what I saw in there?' I was already

coming up with excuses.

"'I saw our new video in there'…

"'I'm sorry Scott'…

"'I saw our video in there and it was AMAZING!'

"Phew! It turned out the guys use Burger King because it does great coffee."

Classic Rock quickly hailed Rival Sons as "the snappily dressed, spiritually inclined, unlikely saviours of American rock" and the same magazine made the band cover stars for their 2014 album 'Great Western Valkyrie'.

"Earache had some amazing connections and they really pushed them hard," relates a clearly impressed Holiday. "Although a lot of astonished journos went: 'This soul-based rock 'n' roll record came from the same label that gave us Napalm Death?', Classic Rock came on board along with a lot of other European magazines.

"Right from the start we decided against trying to sell Rival Sons to the existing Earache fanbase," Tobin stresses. "From past experiences trying to get death metal kids into hardcore techno that was an obvious blind alley – this was a new sound for Earache and there was no point trying to convince Evile fans to like the band."

Things weren't helped by the fact that the band's first UK tour came as support to Judas Priest and Queensrÿche, and then the band played not one but two sets in a single day at the High Voltage Festival in London during the summer of 2011.

"We had only got the band onto the bill as it was part of the Priest/Queensrÿche tour," Tobin admits, "but Rival Sons' set that

> "LUCKILY, RIVAL SONS' MUSICAL AUTHENTICITY AND SONGWRITING PROWESS SPOKE FOR ITSELF."

The Temperance Movement

day was very well received. And later on that day we got word that Electric Wizard weren't gonna make their slot on another stage so the band played again, and of course all those that had watched them earlier in the day, plus all those who had missed them but heard the buzz afterwards turned up for the second set. That really made a big impression with the audience, and also with us because you saw the work ethic and flexibility of the band right there."

"It really didn't take long for things to start to happen," Holiday agrees. "The response to the video for 'Pressure And Time' made me think: 'Wow, this is really going to open up some doors for us'. I found that very interesting."

Earache's effect upon the career of Rival Sons has been considerable. In the UK, each of their four albums for the label has charted higher than its predecessor, 2016's 'Hollow Bones' peaking at Number 13. The label's contacts also put the band before an entirely new audience on the TV show Later With Jools Holland.

In America things were much tougher. Drummer Michael Miley once explained that the band's radio people had been told: "This is the best record I've heard in 25 years, but we can't play it. It doesn't fit our playlist." However, the band are now a firmly established draw in Europe, both as headliners and at all of the major festivals. They were also hand-picked by Black Sabbath to open throughout Black Sabbaths's farewell world tour, after Ozzy and Sharon Osbourne saw them at the LA Classic Rock Awards and fell in love with the band.

In fact, Rival Sons have a few celebrity fans. Comedian Vic Reeves came to hang out with them at London's Classic Rock Awards and again at the Ramblin' Man Fair. Actor Billy Bob Thornton is another fan, as is William Orbit, Madonna's producer. Henry Rollins is also on record as being blown away by what the band does.

"Earache did a great thing with us," Holiday points out. "Our association with them opened up the roster of bands like The Temperance Movement, Blackberry Smoke – they're all bands that I love. And they've done good with them all."

Holiday describes Digby Pearson as "a very interesting character", adding: "We've hung out but I don't know him very well", but the guitarist is certainly full of respect for the achievements of the label's founder.

"Earache Records is testament to how Digby does business, and how he continues to do it," he states. "I thank him for all of the things that he has done for us. He has maintained his business when so many other labels went through fire-sales and died. Over at the major label HQ entire floors of staff were getting fired but meanwhile here's Earache, still putting out records. I can respect that."

In the wake of the success the label had experienced with Rival Sons, Earache quite rightly sought a little more of the same. ▶

Black Sabbath backstage with Rival Sons.

Picture by Ross Halfin.

The Temperance Movement

Blackberry Smoke

Al with Rival Sons

"A MESSAGE FROM MICK JAGGER SAYING THAT HE LOVES THE BAND. NOW THAT'S WHAT I CALL A COMPLIMENT."

A five-piece group blessed with strong musical roots and powered by a positive, forward-thinking attitude, The Temperance Movement hailed from London and Glasgow and had begun to generate a simmering groundswell of appreciation since playing a debut show at London's Water Rats to 100 people. 12 months on the band sold out the 1,000-capacity Scala. Classic Rock trumpeted: "They sound like the Stones-meets Free-and-The Band-crossed-with-The Black Crowes, and fronted by a man who evokes the spirit of Bon Scott with the larynx of 1970s-era Rod Stewart". The message was out and the scramble began.

"We had an email from Earache really, really early on," recalls Paul Sayer, one of The Temperance Movement's guitar players. "All we had at the time was a couple of live videos on YouTube but they got us a lot of attention, including from Planet Rock Radio. The email dialogue with Earache turned into phone calls and from there things moved pretty quickly."

A first meeting between Earache, the group and their manager at the time, Derek Oliver, the former Kerrang! journalist who had previously signed Pantera and Dream Theater in the 1990s, took place in early 2013.

"It went okay – I probably talked too much, and I had the sense that I hadn't really made a big connection with them; they were not too interested," Dan remembers. "Over the coming months I realised that it's just the way they are – quite grounded, guarded and restrained in a lot of ways. I guess the clue is in the band name. I remember Paul said to me very early on that he wanted them to be the 'rock band it was okay for everyone to like' which I took to mean that they wanted to be a band for the common man, for all kind of rock fans. I shared that view."

Throughout the first half of 2013 Tobin attended as many of the band's gigs as possible, looking on as Derek Oliver was succeeded by Larry Mazer, an American who had once represented Kiss and now looked after Lamb Of God among others.

"One Saturday night the band played at the Bodega in Nottingham and did an amazing acapella version of 'Chinese Lanterns', which blew us away," Tobin relates. "They were so good, the harmonies and the sheer emotion that came over. It was very obvious this was the real deal."

However, the band had other suitors, including an imprint of the massive Universal Records umbrella. And when an Earache posse turned up to see the band play at London's Borderline there was a massive industry presence.

Digby urged Dan to pursue the band, accommodating all the manager's requests, offering a very artist-friendly deal in order to make the deal happen. Both agreed that the label's roster needed to change and for Earache to compete their operating procedures had to follow suit.

"What we had," Tobin qualifies, "was a real opportunity to grow things, not to become all glitzy and showbiz and 'major label', but a chance in a professional sense to work with new people, but at a higher level. The major factor was Dig strategically wanting to move Earache away from our Death Metal past."

Whilst on paper the attention of a major appeared mouth-watering, according to Sayer in terms of finance and commitment, what had been placed on the table by the conglomerate wasn't too far removed from what Earache were offering.

"That made it quite straightforward," the guitarist says. "We made a decision based on which label we preferred. And although we didn't meet Digby maybe until just before we signed, we knew Earache as people and liked the things that they were saying."

Of course The Temperance Movement were well aware of Earache's work on behalf of Rival Sons, but they had no real sense of the company's history.

He continues: "At the same time as Planet Rock was playing ▶

our song 'Only Friend' I saw the video for Rival Sons' video for 'Pressure And Time' and Planet Rock was also playing Rival Sons a fair bit too, so that's when I started to see how perhaps it might all tie together."

The deal was signed in, of all places, a restaurant in Northampton before The Temperance Movement played a gig at the Roadmender over the Download Festival weekend of 2013. With a spring in his step, Tobin then headed off to a muddy Donington Park to show Pearson the paperwork.

As well as for The Temperance Movement these were exciting times for Earache, who now had another excellent, up and coming band to work with.

"Within the space of six months we'd been signed and made the A-List [of songs played] on Planet Rock," Paul recalls proudly. "The five of us had all been involved in music for quite a while, in various different bands so it was a proud moment. Huge sums of money hadn't changed hands, but the deal felt like an important part of all of our individual personal progressions.

"It wasn't something that was going to make us rich overnight, nor should it have been because the values of being grounded and an honest reality are core to the band's belief system," he adds. "Now it was time to start doing the work."

Previously recorded in a mere four days before the tying of the contractual knot, the quintet unveiled their debut album, 'The Temperance Movement', via Earache on September 16, 2013. A mere three months after the band had signed the deal the album peaked at Number 12 in the national chart.

"We were out on the road continuously and had worked very hard, but it was tremendously exciting," Paul Sayer acknowledges. "One of the best things about it [the success] was that we knew it wasn't down to luck or being caught up in some kind of whirlwind, it felt like a direct correlation between the effort we'd put in and what we were getting back out from that. That was inspiring."

As a gauge of their progress, the following summer the band was invited to support The Rolling Stones at gigs in Berlin, Düsseldorf and Vienna. This represented a whole different universe to the bands on Earache's roster, but it was about to get better still. A year further down the line, having flown home from

"THE FIRST TIME WE MET THEIR PEOPLE THEY WERE LIKE: 'OOH, IT'S A HEAVY METAL COMPANY.'"

their debut US tour alongside a certain band called Blackberry Smoke, The Temperance Movement re-packed their bags and returned to the States to accept an offer to open for the Stones at the 80,000-capacity Citrus Bowl in Orlando, Florida.

"We got a message: 'Mr. Richards would like to say hello once you're done. He's waiting in his dressing room'," Sayer grins at the memory. "That's something you don't hear every day of the week. When the Stones first booked us for that Florida show a lot of nice stuff came back from their camp, including a message from Mick Jagger saying that he loves the band. Now that's what I call a compliment."

It was all a long way from Earache's early Heresy and Napalm Death gigs at The Mermaid. As well as making return visits to the States, a follow-up album from The Temperance Movement, 'White Bear', was also a Top 20 record in the UK and the band remained signed to Earache.

Incidentally, on the same day that The Temperance Movement agreed to sign with Earache in Northampton, the groundwork for another signing was slipping into place.

"That band was Blackberry Smoke, who Digby had come across and Earache had been courting for a few months," Tobin continues. "Now the band had moved to larger management, the manager wanted to know all about us and why we were interested in Blackberry Smoke. That was the beginning of things moving fast on that band. By February 2014 we were releasing 'The Whippoorwill', and their decision to come on board with Earache was no doubt influenced by Rival Sons and then the immediate chart success of The Temperance Movement."

Formed in Atlanta, Georgia, at the millennium's turn, Southern rockers Blackberry Smoke had already released two full-length albums, the second of which was through Zac Brown's Southern Ground label, by the time that they became entwined with Earache Records in early 2014.

As luck would have it, the quintet had already reached the conclusion that it was time for them to take a step beyond the North American market just as Earache were expanding their roster still further.

"We knew that we needed distribution in the UK because we were already selling records all over Europe via mail order," explains the band's singer Charlie Starr. "We thought it would be nice to find out whether someone was willing to put our albums into the stores so that we could come over and do some touring, and that's what happened."

"The first time we met their people they were like: 'Ooh, it's a heavy metal company'," remembers Al Dawson. "I found much more resistance from their camp than with the Rival Sons guys. In the end I think they hired some English consultants to meet ▶

The Temperance Movement

Wakrat

Vic Reeves, Nancy Sorrell and Rival Sons

Charlie Starr / Blackberry Smoke

Wyatt Wendels (Planet Rock) and
Blackberry Smoke

with Dig and Dan in London, to get a handle on the company, and that's when they began to understand what was going on."

There was already a tenuous connection. Drummer Brit Turner had been a roommate of Kevin Sharp, the vocalist of Brutal Truth who worked in the label's New York office.

"When I first met Kevin he was with college radio and he interviewed a band that Richard Turner, our bass player, and I had been in before the formation of Blackberry Smoke," Turner recalls. "We became fast friends. When Kevin began working for Earache from time to time I would visit him in the office – man, that place was small. It was like when you were at school and someone would put you in a locker for a joke."

Years previous to Blackberry Smoke, Turner had been part of a Thrash band called Nihilist. No relation to the Swedes of the same name, of course, though it is true that that their existence caused LG Petrov and company to switch to Entombed in 1990.

"I suppose that's possible; we did have a song on one of the Metal Blade compilations," considers Turner, "but Entombed are a great band."

In the end, Earache's Al Dawson went to see Blackberry Smoke play a small club in New York, and that's when the Nihilist connection really paid off.

"In my head I was going through the list of reasons why they needed to be on Earache, but going backstage Brit Turner remembered me from hanging out with Kevin [Sharp] and said: 'I've told the band all about you and the label, and that we really should go with you.' It was that easy!

"Dig later told me that the demo of Nihilist [Brit Turner's 1990s Thrash band] had been sitting on his desk for years, he was well aware of them, in fact it's the reason he urged our Swedish band Nihilist to change their name – and they chose Entombed," Dawson laughs, "and 20 years later eventually Brit Turner became an Earache artist with Blackberry Smoke."

"I'd never even heard of Earache Records until we started to work with them," admits Charlie Starr. "When they came to us we knew they had Rival Sons and it seemed as though they were really branching out. They also had The Temperance Movement. Sure, they were a metal label but we were not too fussed about that. If you meet Digby and Dan, they like good music – no matter which genre. They're smart guys and they actually love music; you'd perhaps be surprised how many people that work in the music business don't really like music at all. It's cool to be in business with someone that you can go to a record store with and talk about what you really have in common."

"But you have to go in before Dan or he'll buy up all of the good stuff," quips Turner. "It was the same with Digby, too. Here was a guy you could have an informed conversation with."

Once Starr did a little homework, his respect continued to grow. "They did incredibly well to keep that label going during some very tough times," he says. "Earache have done a great job for us. They're the only group of people who've followed through and done what they promised to do – that's never happened to us before."

The night after Blackberry Smoke played at the Barfly, Earache took them to the Classic Rock Awards at London's Roundhouse. Prior to the ceremony Dan Tobin had arranged with the Classic Rock publisher Chris Ingham that 'Shakin' Hands With the Holy Ghost', the single from 'The Whippoorwill', would be used as the 'walk up' music each time a gong was handed out.

"I didn't say anything but when the first award was handed out the look on the band's faces was a picture," he laughs, "and broke a lot of ice between us, showing that we were thinking ahead and making those cool little connections."

A connection on a far bigger scale was made the same night at the Classic Rock Awards when The Temperance Movement performed a short set. As Phil Campbell began singing, Brit turned to Tobin and smiled:

> "IT'S QUITE POSSIBLE THAT WITHOUT EARACHE NOBODY WOULD KNOW WHO THE FUCK WE ARE."

"Wow, what a great voice". Fast-forward to March of 2014 and Blackberry Smoke were headlining at the Shepherd's Bush Empire in London.

"So I arranged for Luke [Potashnick, guitarist], Nick [Fyfe, bassist] and Paul from the Temperance Movement to come down to the show and meet Blackberry Smoke," Tobin explains. "They got along really well and from that the two bands ended up doing a long USA tour together. So just like the old days, we were joining the dots for all of our bands."

The role of Planet Rock Radio has played its part in the ascent of Blackberry Smoke. As 'The Whippoorwill' threatened to break, at first Earache had discussed submitting 'Six Ways To Sunday' to their playlist, only to go with 'Shakin' Hands With the Holy Ghost' instead, which scored the band a playlist spot.

As with Rival Sons and The Temperance Movement, Blackberry Smoke took off quicker than anybody had dared to hope. Album number three, 'The Whippoorwill', went Top 30, the concert set 'Leave A Scar – North Carolina' fared only slightly less well, and a fourth studio record, 'Holding All The Roses', reached Number 17, giving Earache and Blackberry Smoke three Top 40 albums in the space of less than a year. Better still, 'Like An Arrow', the group's fifth studio record, reached the Top Ten in October 2016, a considerable feat for any rock band and the first time that Earache had managed it in their UK homeland.

"It all seemed to happen really exponentially," observes Brit Turner. "In that calendar year we went from playing to 200 people ▶

The White Buffalo

"THE AMOUNT OF BALLS DISPLAYED BY THE BAND AND EARACHE IN DOING THAT IS INCREDIBLE."

at the Barfly and two gigs later we were headlining the Forum in London, which holds 2,300. That says a lot of how things worked out."

As previously stated by Al Dawson, nobody really foresaw the addition of a singer-songwriter to Earache's roster. Until that point, The White Buffalo, led by their Oregon-born leader Jake Smith, were probably best known for numerous songs featured in the TV series Sons Of Anarchy. They had enjoyed a moderate degree of self-driven success with a mix of hardcore country, Southern rock and deep soul, though that smoothness also carries a punky edge. Surprising, then, that Smith had never even heard of Earache before they knocked at his door three years ago.

"It's amazing that they have evolved from death metal into a whole other area of music," Smith states. "It's super-cool to be a part of their second wave. They are now known for a style that really speaks to people in an emotional sense. I think that's great."

The relationship has been of enormous benefit to artist and label. Prior to signing in 2014 The White Buffalo had played London's 600-capacity Garage, and on his/their most recent visit they headlined Shepherd's Bush Empire, which holds a couple of thousand. "Before that show at the Garage I hadn't played the UK in 12 years, so I had no expectations in terms of my fan-base," he shrugs. "It's quite possible that without Earache nobody would know who the fuck we are."

Earache had a very good idea, however, stepping in to provide a European deal for the well-received 'Love And The Death Of Damnation'. Its follow-up, 'Darkest Darks, Lightest Lights', came out late 2017.

"Jake is among the easiest and most professional artists that we work with," Dan Tobin says. "We feel we are on the same level as him; we have the same ethics, the same way of working."

For his part, Smith responds: "I'm indebted to Earache.

Wakrat

Wormrot and The Grindcore Goat

NEVER MIND the BALLOTS

#generationfucked

26 JULY 2016
BOARD THE BUS FOR WAKRAT ALBUM PLAY BACK
& SMASH THE GRID - BAND PLANT FLAG AT PARL' SQ
BEFORE SPECIAL WAKRAT GIG @ THE BLACK HEART
SPACE LIMITED CONTACT: kule@earache.com
EXTREMELY LIMITED SPACES RSVP ASAP

earache.com/wakrat

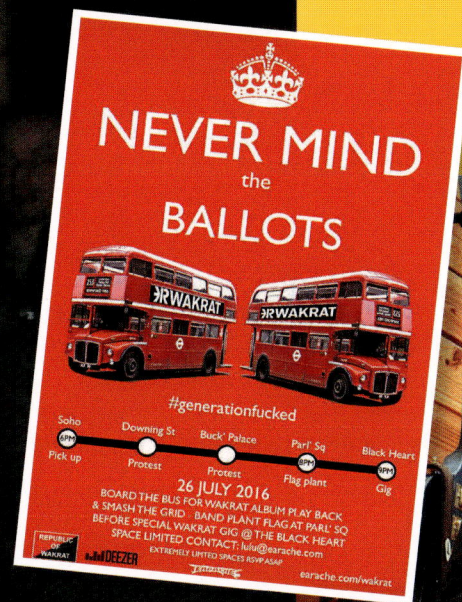

Scott Holiday

I've been doing this for 15 years and neither of us has been an overnight sensation. The relationship has been nothing but a pleasure so far."

Shortly after the signing of The White Buffalo, Earache pulled off another coup, striking a deal with Wakrat, the band featuring Tim Commerford. Previously the bassist of Rage Against The Machine and Audioslave, Commerford is a highly politicised individual. He had clambered to the top of the stage during the live MTV Awards to protest Limp Bizkit winning an award and also appeared naked on stage with RATM with gaffer tape across his mouth.

Clearly, this was just the kind of fascinating character that belonged on Earache Records.

To that end, Earache set up a 'Republic of Wakrat' website at which the band outlines its 'manifesto' and beliefs. In July 2016, Wakrat and Earache staff held a day of protest in Parliament Square, their goal to plant a flag in said Square that officially launched the 'Republic of Wakrat'. Having arrived on a double-decker London bus with the words 'Generation Fucked' down its side Commerford led the way, chanting 'Generation Fucked' at the top of his voice through a megaphone.

"The amount of balls displayed by the band and Earache in doing that is incredible," Tobin claims. "Of course security came over and tried to stop us, but for a good 15 mins we carried on."

After the protest, everyone returned to the bus only to find it had broken down. It was abandoned outside the Houses Of Parliament, complete with slogan in massive letters, for about six hours. This was a key moment because months later when the Glastonbury Festival team visited Nottingham to discuss the idea of the Earache's involvement at this year's event, they were impressed with the absolute nerve of the thing; the political nature, and the confrontational approach taken by the label. ♠

Napalm Death

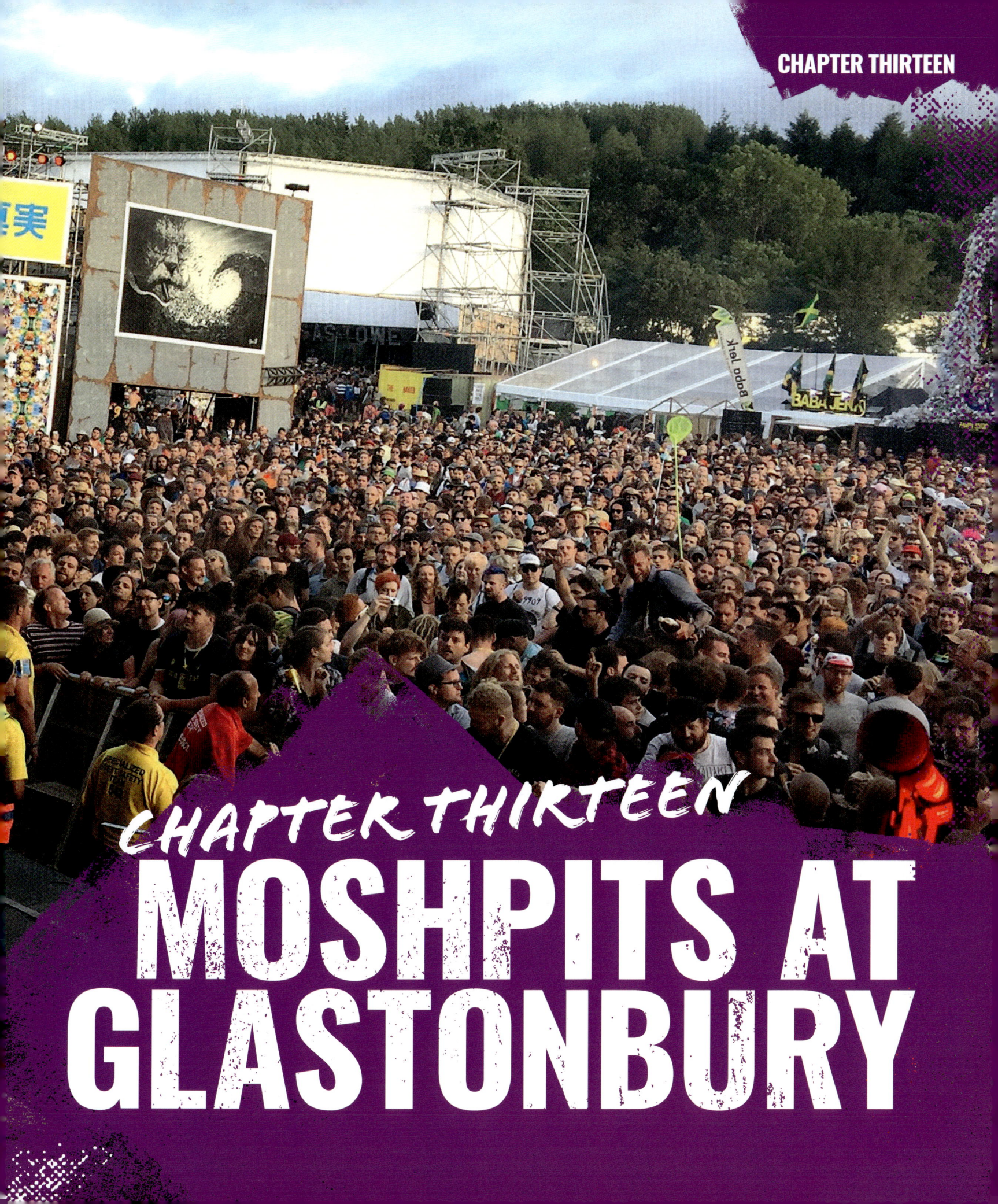

CHAPTER THIRTEEN

MOSHPITS AT GLASTONBURY

When Blackberry Smoke played at Glastonbury Festival in 2016 and were watched by organiser Michael Eavis, Earache decided to chance their arm and propose the idea of putting on some heavier acts.

"Tom Hadfield pestered Eavis for a while asking why he never books heavy bands and after a while he just walked off – fair enough, Metallica and others have played at Glastonbury," Tobin recalls of that first encounter. "But Digby was determined to plug away, he was certain Earache belonged at Worthy Farm, our ideals aligned so much."

"Tom Hadfield, our newest and youngest staffer, struck up the subject of why metal was being ignored by a festival of contemporary arts," Digby Pearson explains. "Our proposal to help them book heavier bands was dismissed out of hand at first – but they took a chance on us."

Following another approach in March 2017, mere months before the event was due to happen, the powers-that-be introduced Earache to Chris Tofu who curates Shangri-La, the most open-minded field at Glastonbury.

"Shangri-La is a place where reggae, dubstep, house, techno, brass bands and radical politics all share space in the most electrifying late night mash-up/sound clash atmosphere possible," Pearson says. "There are seven stages, run barely metres apart. The place is wild, borderline feral, and comes alive when the main stages close and the festivities run throughout the night."

When Glasto's eventual proposal came in, Earache were taken aback. The invitation allowed them to book some bands for the Truth stage and also curate their own area – a disused 60-foot London Underground tube carriage, housed in Shangri-La. At first the idea of putting on live music within the carriage was batted back for health and safety reasons, though finally the Glastonbury team allowed it.

Although the band had left the label in acrimonious circumstances at the end of the previous millennium, Earache knew right way that they wanted to put Napalm Death onto the Truth stage, mostly because they felt they belonged there but also as Tobin puts it, as "a rather nice olive branch". Fortuitously, Shane Embury happened to be in Nottingham on the day after the proposal was made. Having dropped in for a cuppa at Chez Tobin, very little persuasion was required.

"Shane moaned that Napalm Death are never asked to play at the Reading or Leeds Festivals, and of course he was right," Dan says. "They realised very quickly that accepting would do them a lot of good. For my part, I buffed it out that I'd get them onto the TV, which as it turns out is exactly what happened."

Awareness of the label's 30th anniversary escalated stratospherically when, during the build-up to Glastonbury, Napalm Death found an unlikely presence on Radio 2 as Barney Greenway provided a live on-air lesson in the fine art of extreme metal growling to none other than Ed Miliband, the former leader of the Labour Party and, it would seem, a genuine admirer of the group. YouTube went haywire.

Band and label were aware that this could have been cheesy, but as Greenway says: "I was surprised to discover that Miliband is a Napalm Death fan. He was au fait with the band's music and also of our whole ethos."

With a month to go, Glastonbury had second thoughts, believing it unsafe for bands to play in the carriage and almost pulled the plug, though in the end a line-up that also included Earache's group of artists – including Extreme Noise Terror, former Sex Pistol Glen Matlock, Wormrot, New Jersey noiseniks Ho99o9 and Steve Ignorant's Slice Of Life – all got to perform, despite the fact that 15 minutes before Matlock's set was due to commence their health and safety team were still installing a makeshift additional emergency exit.

"The men with clipboards arrived and said: 'What the fuck's going on here?'" Tom Hadfield says. "And all the time, Glen is standing there and tapping his watch. Even as he began the first song they were still working on the stage. Jamie, one of our guys, was literally gaffer taping this scaffolding together."

The line-up of the Earache Express was completed mere days before the festival began, and the site was still in the very early stages of being built when the label's employees arrived.

"It was awe inspiring to watch a temporary city being built

> **"THE PLACE IS WILD, BORDERLINE FERAL, AND COMES ALIVE WHEN THE MAIN STAGES CLOSE."**

▶

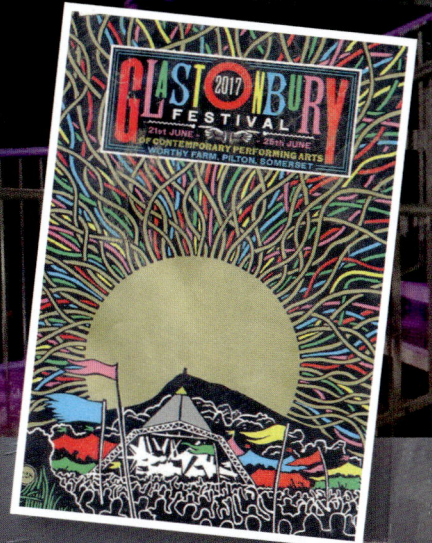

Earache Express stage at Glastonbury

Dig with LG Petrov (Entombed)

Earache Glastonbury Crew with Steve Ignorant (Crass)

from nothing in a field which once held cows," says Pearson. "This year the theme was recycling and huge mounds of leftover clothes and plastic bottles from 2016's festival were sculpted into pyramids to remind us to take our trash home."

"Even as we pulled up at the gates we were still scratching our heads that this was actually happening," Greenway admits. "It's the biggest festival out there and we are a 'noise' band – why would anyone book a band that isn't very summery? This is very sonically violent music."

Hiccoughs were many and varied, from the 35-degree heatwave that made the inside of the tube unbearable to a lack of passes for working personnel.

Pearson was happy to meet a convivial Barney Greenway backstage. "It was literally the first time we'd spoken in 20 years, any animosity from the past disappeared instantly as we hugged and had a quick chat, mostly about how the band was going, his move to Brighton and how he still loved the Villa," Dig chuckles. "Selfies were taken; it was empowering to be back on the same wavelength."

Coming just a couple of weeks after the Grenfell Tower fire disaster had claimed the lives of more than 80 innocents, Barney's between-song rants about slum landlords, international borders, zero-hour contracts and GM crops ("Everyone deserves a life of dignity and happiness," he insisted, introducing the band's remake of Dead Kennedys' 'Nazi Punks Fuck Off'), connected with the crowd, distilling the very essence of Napalm Death – take it or leave it. Earache staffer Lucy Hellings gave the BBC a running commentary side-stage, and although some reports made glib use of his quip of: "If you're not following, lyric sheets can be obtained" there was an air of respect for the real message.

"We absolutely would not treat that gig any differently than playing to fifty people in Huddersfield on a Tuesday night," Greenway states. "Doing so would be a betrayal of those fifty people, who are the ones we need the most. We certainly didn't alter our set to make it – quote-unquote – listenable."

In the end, there were huge queues to get into the 15,000-capacity Shangri-La field as Napalm Death played, and the carriage was so populated over the weekend that a one person in and one out system had to be employed.

"To me, it felt as though Grindcore was receiving some kind of formal acceptance. So often we've had to justify it in the past; it does have a lot to say, and here were Napalm Death talking in letters that were ten feet high," says Dan Tobin.

Earache at Glasto was indeed a massive success. Napalm Death appeared live on BBC2 at teatime on TV, sandwiched between Liam Gallagher and Foo Fighters, placing them in front of millions of viewers. Another overwhelming positive was

Wormrot

Dig with Barney Greenway (Napalm Death)

Wormrot in tube carriage

"NAPALM DEATH APPEARED LIVE ON BBC2 AT TEATIME ON TV, SANDWICHED BETWEEN LIAM GALLAGHER AND THE FOO FIGHTERS."

that it warmed relations between Earache and Napalm Death.

Tobin reflects on the whole Earache at Glastonbury experience. "It's one of the best things the label has ever done," he believes. "It took a monumental effort for about six staffers to make it work. We literally did it all from manning the bar to deejaying, stewarding and security, but somehow we made it all happen for the bands, who unanimously voiced appreciation, and for the label and the scene."

2018 marked a fallow year for the festival but Earache returned with a larger presence at the 2019 Glastonbury/Shangri-La festival curating an entire stage for heavy music called "Scum" plus booked the likes of Denzel Curry and Gojira for the larger Truth stage. Entombed AD played with LG Petrov on vocals, further cementing the ever-growing link between Earache's past and current activities.

"That was surreal; I could never have dreamed of playing something like that. We were playing on the same bill as the Bee Gees!" laughs Wormrot guitarist Rasyid Juraimi of the band's Glastonbury 2017 experience. "We were hoping for something special and a huge crowd showed up. It was absolutely crazy!"

Crazy, certainly, but perhaps not quite as crazy the now

infamous occasion when, at a gig on farmland, Biquette the goat decided to take a front-row position as the band stormed through their set.

"You want to talk about the goat?" Rasyid Juraimi laughs.

Yep. The grindcore goat has since become a viral sensation online.

"In October 2010 we played a gig at a squat in Villeneuve, France, that also had a farm on the land, so there were a load of animals there. There was a goat who was so friendly towards us, like a domestic pet. She followed us around all day, messing up our luggage, lying on our beds. So we played, and the room was really cold and people were in the corners huddling together, and then we saw this goat coming in from the corner and she stood in front of us. Our singer was petting her and singing to her while we were playing!"

Pulling Earache back from the precipice of extinction, the past few years have been astonishingly successful. Had the label not elected to diversify and with the market shrinking and changing so drastically, one can only wonder whether the company as we know it might have ceased to be.

"That's entirely possible, and those that work here may have ▶

Crowd outside of Earache Express

Reminding people to recycle

thought it, but never said it," acknowledges Dan Tobin. "However, the label's ability to plough on regardless suggests that we'd still exist. There was no great plan for us to do what we did, that's just not how we work.

"I do know that I myself had got to the point where I was sick of working with death metal and thrash," he points out. "There was a ceiling to what we were doing and I was becoming pissed off with bands that are quitters – those that make a couple of albums and then split up at the first hurdle."

Certainly, there is no going back.

"It was obvious from an early stage with Rival Sons that we couldn't return to the type of acts we had signed in the last millennium," Tobin states. "And what the experiences with The Temperance Movement and Blackberry Smoke have shown is that our achievements with Rival Sons were not a fluke or luck.

"I firmly believe that all those years chipping away by selling Carcass, or Napalm Death or Godflesh – those bands are a hard sell, globally – those times stood us in good stead when working campaigns with bands that had a chance of getting onto the radio and TV. Basically we had learned the business the hard way."

Dan Tobin already notes a sea-change away from the blues rock of the label's most recent releases. "There's still more to come from the genre," he says, "but when you see other labels jumping on the bandwagon then its shelf-life must be coming to an end. The same thing happened with death metal. When you've had Entombed, Morbid Angel and Carcass at the height of their game putting out genre-defining records, then why put up with a bunch of second-rate impersonators?

"In a broader sense, I believe that Earache should continue to diversify as far as we dare," he adds.

More frustrating still, Tobin elaborates by way of a postscript to the above, is the crop of bands that were signed to Earache, sold very few records at the time and then went on to prosper later elsewhere. He cites Sleep, Clutch and At The Gates as examples. Relationships have in some instances suffered. But such is life.

Other bands have split up, found themselves celebrated by a crop of wide-eyed newbies and been tempted by a second bite of the cherry. Again, this doesn't always result in band-label harmony.

"This might sound big headed, but we consider that we kept the catalogues of those bands going by repacking and re-promoting them," Tobin claims. "It's easy for a band like Carcass to walk back in and pick up where they left off after a decade away, because we had never let those records die. The bands will insist that it was their great work that kept the doors open [for a reunion] – the real truth probably lies somewhere in between, but of course we don't get any credit for that.

"I can't pretend it's easy to see a band that you've spotted and

Michael Eavis (Glastonbury Founder) with Tom Hadfield

" HIS SINGLE-MINDEDNESS IS WHAT'S GOT US THIS FAR. "

Extinction Rebellion boat

nurtured when nobody else gave a shit... A case in point would be Entombed," he continues. "That band gets bigger than anyone envisaged and the major labels start sniffing. When they tell you that you're doing a shit job and they'd like to fuck off… wait a minute, we don't agree with that. It's a horrible feeling and it's unfair."

There were times a decade ago, he admits, when he sat down with Pearson to ponder a list of bills that required settling. "Dig would put a line through them one by one and say: 'That'll have to wait. I haven't got the money'. We liked to think that we could always A&R our way out of any potential problem."

Along the way Earache's reinvention has stirred up its fair share of haters, though in the grand scheme of things such internet bleatings are inconsequential. Meanwhile, the label goes from strength to strength.

"As a record company's staff gets older shouldn't its taste in music change?" reasons the company's former A&R man Hugh Jones. "The guys at Earache must be in their fifties now? I'm sure they don't listen to the exactly same stuff they did in the 1980s. Does anyone?"

"I give Dig every credit in the world for keeping a truly independent record company going for all this time," Dan adds. "He's too bloody minded [to stop] and he can't stand being told what to do by anybody. His single-mindedness is what's got us this far." ♠

Earache Express staff

Digby Pearson.

CHAPTER FOURTEEN
PIONEER SPIRIT

Picture by Mark Leary.

Formal marks of acceptance have been few and far between, though in 2015 Pearson won the Pioneer Award at the Association Of Independent Music Awards, marking a 30 year career at the cutting edge of metal and rock music. Previous winners were the founders of Mute, Rough Trade, Domino, and later XL and Warp, thus placing Pearson in the exalted company of the legendary founders of the UK independent music scene. "I was very honoured to receive the award, it was about time metal and rock were recognised by the industry to be honest, it's a reward for team work of all the staffers past and present - it's a team effort at the coal face every day." Dig commented.

"During my time at the label Dig was always great to work with," says Hugh Jones now. "He took a lot of shit back in the 1990s but never bothered to defend himself and because of that he's perceived as a little… reclusive? But in the long run he made all the best decisions. Had he listened [to the cynics] Earache would have gone out of business a long time ago. He's very sharp and he's got a good ear for music."

"I'm very happy for Earache that their success has continued," comments Benji Webbe. "It's great that they've signed so many interesting new bands."

"The label tried to reinvent itself in the mid-1990s with Dub War and did okay with that but, they have really achieved the goal with the likes of Rival Sons," adds Gaz Jennings. "I'm chuffed for them."

"I will always think of Earache as being so far ahead of their time," concludes Andy Copping. "Dig and his team almost invented genres before they became reality. Pitchshifter were a blueprint for The Prodigy and they also had a band called Ultraviolence who played a violently aggressive mix of techno and industrial music long before that became popular. They had Dub War who evolved into Skindred. They had that Norwegian guy Mortiis – a guy wearing a mask way before Slipknot.

"It's too easy to say that Earache were the forefathers of grindcore and death metal because now they've pushed the boundaries further than ever with Rival Sons, Blackberry Smoke, The Temperance Movement, White Buffalo, and all the rest – those acts are all very different to the label's usual staple diet.

"Sure, there was the dalliance with Columbia Records but apart from that they've retained their independence, stayed true to what they believe in and remained in Nottingham, and thirty years on the story continues. I've got nothing but respect for the label." ♠

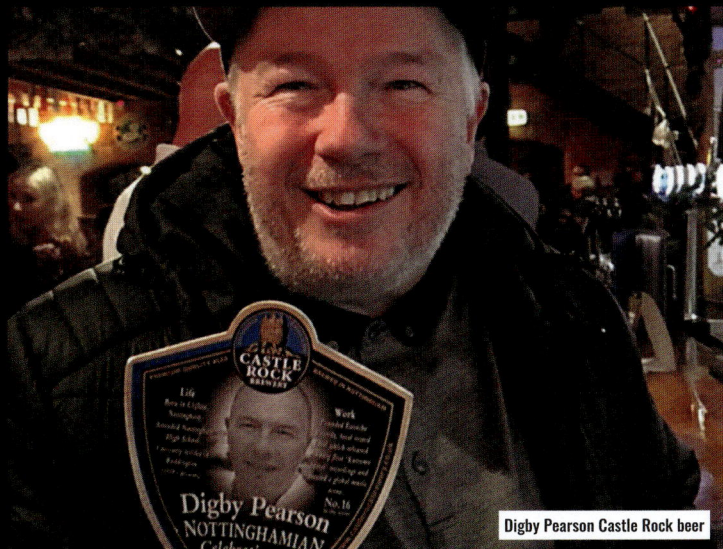

Digby Pearson Castle Rock beer

Dig with Andy Copping at Download Festival

Scarlet Rebels

CHAPTER FIFTEEN
FESTIVALS &
ROCK N' ROLL

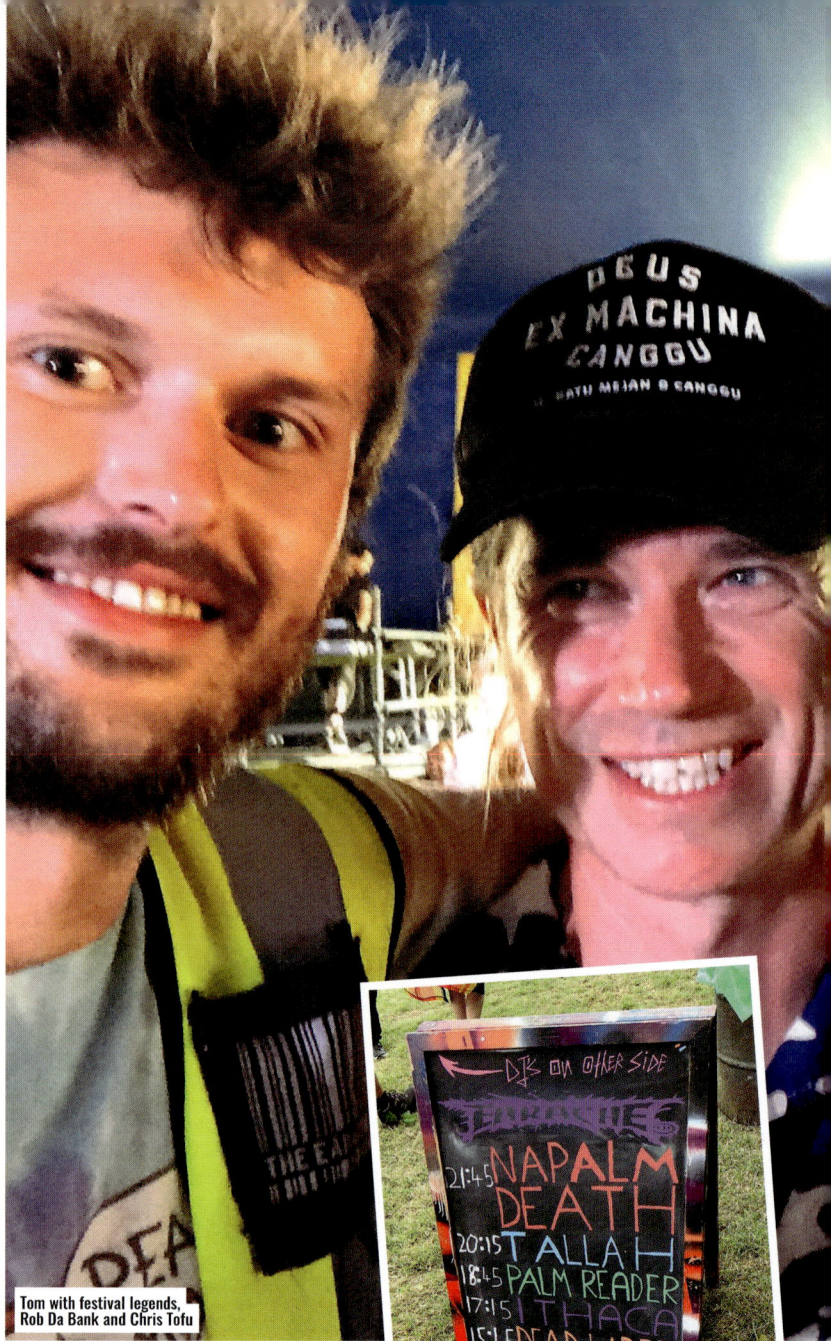

his book was originally written and completed in 2017 but remained unpublished.

Fast-forward to 2022 and the success of Earache's Glastonbury stage took everyone by surprise. For the label, it opened up a new path; the label was in demand to curate a similar stage for heavy music at other festivals in the UK.

"We did our second festival stage in 2018 at Boomtown," says Tom Hadfield, Label Manager and Head Of Live, "and this was the next level, because we went from this train carriage with a few spots on to a bigger stage to having this whole stage bill. It was Boomtown's 10th festival, and they created an incredible stage-set - The Earache Factory - which was conceived to resemble an old military installation with a 2,000 capacity. They really went all out on the set design, basically building this fictional city!"

With the likes of Dead Kennedys, Earth Crisis and Soulfly laying waste to Boomtown, another feather in Earache's Festival Cap was with a stage at Camp Bestival in Dorset. Run by Rob Da Bank, the festival is geared more towards families with young children rather than dedicated moshers. As Tom says, "we were walking around the night before and I thought we'd pushed it too far; we saw all these families and went pale! 'What have we done?'," he laughs. "But it was great. Napalm seems to be a band that everyone wants to say they've seen, and so out of nowhere this huge crowd of families turned up. A mosh pit broke out of kids in superhero costumes!"

Perhaps most pleasingly, the festivals demonstrated that the bridges between the label and their legacy acts had not been entirely burned, with luminaries such as Napalm, Godflesh, At The Gates and Lawnmower Deth accepting invitations to play alongside hosts of other names old and new.

Earache renamed as Scum stage at Shangri-La for Glastonbury 2019, which hosted Idles, Gojira and Denzel Curry plus a tribute to Keith Flint of The Prodigy whose death in March of that year came as a huge shock to the festival scene. We wanted

Tom with festival legends, Rob Da Bank and Chris Tofu

The Dust Coda at Top Gear track

"WE'VE BEEN MAKING IT AN ABSOLUTE MISSION TO GET OUR BANDS IN THE CHARTS AS HIGH AS POSSIBLE"

The Dust Coda

MUSIC FOR THE PRODIGAL GENERATION

A KEITH FLINT TRIBUTE

to pay tribute, as Label Manager Dan Hardingham explains: "We filled the screens with video montages of Keith, it was phenomenal - absolutely amazing. DJ Mike Freear was on fire for the 'Keith Flint Appreciation Hour', between 4am-5am, 7000 people raving as the sun was rising. It was beautiful; honestly, it was hugely magical and emotional. Mike poured his heart and soul into the set and so many gathered to pay tribute. When I got back to the office, I had an email from The Prodigy's management with only one word, 'Respect'."

This avenue of adventure was sadly curtailed by the Coronavirus pandemic that, in the early months of 2020, rapidly swept across the globe. Such was the level of hospitalisations and deaths at the time that governments worldwide instituted mass lockdowns and other restrictions that immediately curtailed any and all live performances, putting not only the festivals on hold but also threatening the livelihoods of so many involved in almost every last facet of the music business. At the same time, the unexpected departure of long-term Label Manager Dan Tobin in 2020 for pastures new meant Earache had to adapt very quickly to new working conditions, as well as staff changes. The 'Adapt Or Die' slogan (and original title of this book) went from being a cool motto to actual real life.

An immediate problem faced by the label was an enforced working from home policy that saw all but essential workers mandated to only leave their homes for groceries and a daily stroll.

"I thought Dig would be completely anti-everyone working from home. I just thought he wouldn't be having it at all," laughs Dan Hardingham, "and he would get us back in at the first opportunity because the office has always been quite rigid."

"Even if you've been out until 4 or 5am with bands, Dig would expect you in the office at 10am on the dot the following day," smiles Al Dawson.

The Earache Factory at Boomtown

Goodbye June

The Dust Coda signing

GOODBYE JUNE
See Where The Night Goes

Massive Wagons

"But it was quite the opposite. He sent us all home a week before it was officially the advice to and ever since then, it's basically, 'cool; carry on working at home'," adds Dan.

"I think we basically went out of our way to prove that just because we were at home, it didn't mean that we couldn't operate like we did before; I don't think it's wrong to say really that we've almost gotten up a level in terms of our output. Since we've been working from home, we've had some really mega success with chart positions and stuff like that.

"Bands haven't been able to tour or go to record stores to do signing sessions, so we've had to completely rethink the way we do promotion. In many ways we've been incredibly lucky because we're surrounded by booking agencies and venues that have seen devastation; their businesses just completely disappeared for two years. We managed to avoid that, and Dig didn't put any of us on furlough."

Faced with a potential decimation of both their livelihoods and those of their bands, Earache adopted a two-pronged approach; for their artists, the label encouraged them to maintain as close a contact with their audience as possible, whether through podcasts or social media ("Those Damn Crows did their CrowCast; there's been over eighty episodes so far. It's been so successful. They get different celebrities on and it's really taken on a life of its own," Dan enthuses), while Earache themselves continued to revisit their legacy catalogue with a continued Full Dynamic Range

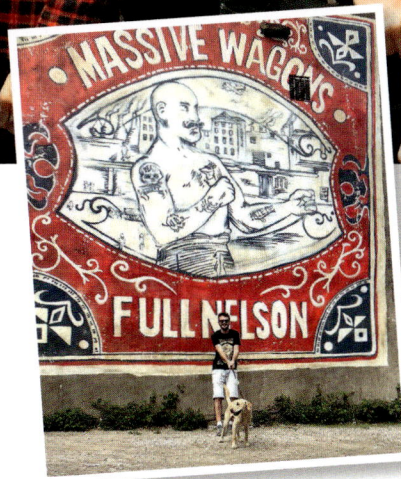

vinyl campaign, while also going all out to break their latest signings. Those efforts, for both the roster and for the label itself, have not been without commercial success; recent releases have seen incredibly high first-week chart placings off the back of innovative, some might even say guerrilla marketing campaigns, alongside fans who, unable to go to gigs, decided to support bands by buying physical releases and merchandise, placing a new breed of Rock n' Roll bands like The Dust Coda and Goodbye June in the UK Top 40, and propelled Welsh firebrands Scarlet Rebels into the UK Top 10 at an astonishing Number 7 first week. The very notion of a chart placing is, in itself, a testament to Earache's 'Adapt Or Die' philosophy. Back in the label's heyday the label might just scrape a Top 50 or 75 chart placing for Carcass or Napalm Death and, back then, that in itself was a huge achievement.

"Since I've been here, we've honed and refined our technique of promotion, and we've been making it an absolute mission to get our bands in the charts as high as possible by getting pre-orders as high as we can," says Tom Hadfield. "One example was Massive Wagons and their 'Full Nelson' album. We had an idea to do a mural of the album artwork somewhere in Lancaster. There was a venue, The Pub in Lancaster, who were friendly with the band as they played there a few times. They agreed to let us do this huge mural on the side of their pub! We sorted that out, ▶

Earache staff with Ryan Richards at the Music Week Awards

Boomtown crew

rented a cherry picker, hired an artist and it caused quite a stir. The local council said it was an unauthorised advert and tried to get it removed. But the Massive Wagons fans started a petition that got eight thousand signatures. BBC Radio Lancashire were supposed to have an interview with a councillor but he bottled it and didn't show up. But for us it meant a band from Lancaster got national attention and we managed to chart them."

In line with the off-the-wall promotional campaigns, other ideas for promotion and merchandise were formulated and executed, culminating in an action figure based on the demon in Napalm Death's 'Scum' album artwork, manufactured by Super7.

"During lockdown we started making gym wear, hot sauce, Grindcore coffee, all sorts of things," says Dan Hardingham. "A few years prior to that I had been looking at creating figures of our most important acts. I spoke with factories all over the world and even independent artists, but Super7 came through and loved the idea of making a 'Scum' demon action figure, based on Napalm Death's legendary 'Scum' album, which the band and their manager signed off on also. I worked closely with the Super7 team and they were amazing; so passionate about getting every detail right, even creating a scuzzy feel for the packaging. The Napalm Death figure sits alongside figures of Metallica, Slayer, Megadeth, Motörhead, all classic, iconic bands - that says it all, really!"

Earache has also made great strides in the publishing and sync realm. Publishing Manager Jeni Lambert explains: "Whilst it can seem like a losing battle against the giant major label machine where songs are specifically produced with sync placements in mind, Earache holds this great niche of a) truly authentic music and b) being the place to go for pioneering metal and rock. We've seen to Rival Sons being placed in a Hyundai advert, alt Nottingham duo Haggard Cat becoming the first ever rock band used in a revolutionary app Apollo, where gamers can soundtrack their Fortnite games with the band's music, Sleep were sync'd in a Nicole Kidman movie 'Destroyer', and Napalm Death's "You

Suffer" even appeared in the TV show 'Silicon Valley' multiple times in one episode!" Additionally, the label recently diversified into Earache Digital Distribution (EDD) and the world of artist management.

"For many of our bands, they'd call us and ask things like 'can you get an agent, and get us a van for the tour?'," says Al Dawson, "so we were already doing a lot of duties that managers were doing in the first place, and we did it because it's in our vested interest to build the band up as much as possible. But I had a conversation with a friend who is both a label head and a manager, who won't sign a band unless she's managing them. I thought that was a conflict of interest, but she said that many times a band and a label have a great working relationship and then certain managers or certain people from types of management school will create a rift between the two, almost to look like they are earning their commission.

"So I was talking with Tallah, who we had just signed, who said 'we want you to be our manager'. I was a little taken aback and I talked to Dig about it. He said, 'Well, you know what? That's actually a really good idea. Let's try it'. So, we started doing it and so far, so good. I mean, it is weird at times when you're beating up the staff accountant over the royalty statements. You know, 'hey, what is this?' 'What's this charge on their statement for?', but it makes sense."

"Yes, there's been some awkward things because of the quite different roles," says Tom Hadfield. "I'm the manager, not the label guy or the other way around. I have to be the manager guy who needs to get money out of the label to do stuff which causes a bit of friction," he laughs, "but it's working well, so far. I think the main thing is that Dig signed those bands so he believes in them. He only really backs bands he thinks are something quite special."

Whether it has been Mighty Force or John Zorn or Scorn to Grindcore or Dub War and Nasenbluten following Death Metal, Earache's ability to left-turn from what many consider to be their niche market has played out again in recent times, with the move

Bob Vylan at Glastonbury 2022

Picture by Nathan Roach

into blues rock being firmly juxtaposed by Dig's interest in Trap; seeing in it the fire and 'fuck you' to the establishment that no doubt provided the spark for many of the label's early signings and ultimately leading to the label signing London's BVDLVD .

"We've gone after a number of people," says Dan Hardingham. "Dig and I went to see Ghostemane in a support slot at The Underworld in London in 2017. He was really good, but it didn't happen. Dig loves extreme things, and it doesn't matter what it is. It's like, the more extreme the better, you know? I can see there are lots of similarities between Trap and the DIY punk world.

"Tom and I went to see 6ix9ine in East London the same year, his manager invited us to join him at a strip bar in Soho afterwards. I wasn't having that at all," he laughs, "as I knew he was with his entourage and it would be my credit card getting a hammering! We were also interested in ZillaKami and City Morgue, that whole scene. We've finally got our own signing with BVDLVD; we haven't released anything yet but that will be a big surprise for people, I'm sure."

"We talked to loads of unsigned Trap guys and they just sit at home on the computer all day long," says Al Dawson. "They make the tracks, they get on Instagram and just hustle. One kid we were talking to was making $75,000 a year just through DIYing it. These guys have half a million monthly listeners and their fans pretty much live on the internet. What got Ghostemane on our radar was the fact that he was using Darkthrone samples and stuff like that. It's a really interesting mix of genres. You look at Mick Harris and Scorn and the transition from that to Bass music to

Dig and Justin Broadrick (Godflesh)

Those Damn Crows

"DIG RECOGNISES EARACHE'S DNA IN THE TRAP SCENE— IT'S TRUE STREET MUSIC."

Al with 6ix9ine's management

Tallah

Tom and ZillaKami

Trap; there's a distinct line there, Dig recognises Earache's DNA in the Trap scene, it's true street music."

While Dig's vision is most certainly focused on the future and the possibilities that it might bring, there has also been, of late, something of a reflection and a renaissance of the past. On one level, Earache got the chance to release one of the staff's collective all-time favourite albums when the legendary 'Walk Among Us' album by the equally legendary Misfits was picked up for a European release and assigned the coveted MOSH666 catalogue number.

"We had a general manager come in who had a really good relationship with Warner, and Dig said that he should try and license some stuff. We picked out lots of things but the top one we wanted was 'Walk Among Us'. We were all huge Misfits fans; Dig has all the original singles, and I have been obsessed with them for years. I flew to the US to see them reunited a couple of times; I saw them at a sold-out Madison Square Gardens. To have an involvement in their discography had me doing back flips!" says Dan Hardingham.

"We took the audio from the original master tapes for our re-issue and introduced the green logo on pink cover; being collectors we knew what people wanted. The first orders on our webstore got a free art card from the Cave session shoot shot in 1981 by Eerie Von."

It's a distant echo of the label's roots when Dig sold and traded early Misfits 7 inch records, and corresponded with Pushead who drew early Misfits flyers and helped Earache early on.

While Wormrot have held the Grindcore banner high for the label for several years now ("We're conscious of those bands, especially with a label as legendary as Earache," says Rasyid Juraimi. "The pressure of expectation we feel to make records as good as that standard is hard, but we do try to do our own thing."), 2022 has seen the return of the legendary Terrorizer to the label's fold, alongside Dub War. "It's great to see them back," says Tom Hadfield.

Finally Digby sums up his 35 year journey: "I'm not a nostalgia person normally, but just the act of putting this book together has been a real trip, reminiscing about the bands, rummaging through dusty photo archives, the memories are flooding back, it's been an amazing ride. At the end of the day the fact we're still operating independently and not bowing down to corporate paymasters is all down to the fans who follow and support the label in all its myriad of twists and turns."

He has brought the story of Earache full circle to the juxtaposition of grind and genre boundary-pushing that has been, is and always shall be the label's calling card. ♠

CHAPTER SIXTEEN

HAVE YOU MET AL?

EARACHE RECORDS
STAY SAFE
MAKE AMERICA RAGE AGAIN
IN GRIND WE ROT
AVIS
GODFLESH

35
EARACHE
YEARS OF NOISE